BRITISH RAILW,

LOCO

CW00550230

FORTY-NINTH EDITION
2007

The Complete Guide to all
Locomotives which operate on
National Rail and Eurotunnel

Robert Pritchard & Peter Fox

ISBN 1 902336 51 8

© 2006. Platform 5 Publishing Ltd., 3 Wyvern House, Sark Road, Sheffield,
S2 4HG, England.

CONTENTS

PROVISION OF INFORMATION

This book has been compiled with care to be as accurate as possible, but in some cases official information is not available and the publisher cannot be held responsible for any errors or omissions. We would like to thank the companies and individuals which have been co-operative in supplying information to us. The authors of this series of books are always pleased to receive notification from readers of any inaccuracies readers may find in the series, to enhance future editions. Please send comments to:

Robert Pritchard, Platform 5 Publishing Ltd., 3 Wyvern House, Sark Road, Sheffield, S2 4HG, England.
Tel: 0114 255 2625   **Fax:** 0114 255 2471
e-mail: robert@platform5.com

This book is updated to 16 October 2006.

UPDATES

This book is updated to the Stock Changes given in **Today's Railways UK 60** (December 2006). Readers are therefore advised to update this book from the official Platform 5 Stock Changes published every month in **Today's Railways UK** magazine, starting with issue 61.

The Platform 5 magazine **Today's Railways UK** contains news and rolling stock information on the railways of Britain and Ireland and is published on the second Monday of every month. For further details of **Today's Railways UK**, please see the advertisement on the back cover of this book.

BRITAIN'S RAILWAY SYSTEM

INFRASTRUCTURE & OPERATION

Britain's national railway infrastructure is owned by a "not for dividend" company, Network Rail. Many stations and maintenance depots are leased to and operated by Train Operating Companies (TOCs), but some larger stations remain under Network Rail control. The only exception is the infrastructure on the Isle of Wight, which is nationally owned and is leased to the Island Line franchisee.

Trains are operated by TOCs over Network Rail, regulated by access agreements between the parties involved. In general, TOCs are responsible for the provision and maintenance of the locomotives, rolling stock and staff necessary for the direct operation of services, whilst Network Rail is responsible for the provision and maintenance of the infrastructure and also for staff needed to regulate the operation of services.

DOMESTIC PASSENGER TRAIN OPERATORS

The large majority of passenger trains are operated by the TOCs on fixed term franchises. Franchise expiry dates are shown in parentheses in the list of franchisees below:

Franchise	Franchisee	Trading Name
Central Trains[1]	National Express Group plc (until 11 November 2007)	Central Trains
Chiltern Railways	M40 Trains Ltd. (until July 2021)	Chiltern Railways
Cross-Country[2]	Virgin Rail Group Ltd. (until 11 November 2007)	Virgin Trains
Gatwick Express[3]	National Express Group plc (until 27 April 2011)	Gatwick Express
Greater Western[4]	First Group plc (until 31 March 2013)	First Great Western
Greater Anglia[5]	National Express Group plc (until 31 March 2011)	"One"
Integrated Kent[6]	GoVia Ltd. (Go-Ahead/Keolis) (until 31 March 2012)	Southeastern
InterCity East Coast[7]	GNER Holdings Ltd. (until 30 April 2012)	Great North Eastern Railway
InterCity West Coast	Virgin Rail Group Ltd. (until 8 March 2012)	Virgin Trains
Island Line[8]	Stagecoach Holdings plc (until 3 February 2007)	Island Line
LTS Rail	National Express Group plc (until 25 May 2011)	c2c
Merseyrail Electrics[9]	Serco/NedRail (until 20 July 2028)	Merseyrail Electrics

Midland Main Line[10]	National Express Group plc (until 11 November 2007)	Midland Mainline
North London Railways[11]	National Express Group plc (until 11 November 2007)	Silverlink Train Services
Northern Rail[12]	Serco/NedRail (until 11 September 2013)	Northern
ScotRail	First Group plc (until 16 October 2011)	First ScotRail
South Central	GoVia Ltd. (Go-Ahead/Keolis) (until December 2009)	Southern
South Western[8]	Stagecoach Holdings plc (until 3 February 2007)	South West Trains
Thameslink/Great Northern[13]	First Group plc (until 31 March 2012)	First Capital Connect
Trans-Pennine Express	First Group/Keolis (until 31 January 2012)	First Trans-Pennine Express
Wales & Borders	Arriva Trains Ltd. (until 6 December 2018)	Arriva Trains Wales

Notes:

[1] Due to be abolished on expiry. Services to be split between the new East Midlands franchise (also incorporating the existing Midland Mainline franchise and part of Cross-Country) and West Midlands franchises (including all existing West Midlands area Central Trains and Silverlink services). Chiltern Railways have been asked to submit a separate proposal to operate the existing Birmingham Snow Hill Central Trains services.

[2] A new expanded Cross-Country franchise will be created from November 2007, also including the existing Central Trains Birmingham–Stansted Airport and Nottingham–Hereford/Cardiff services.

[3] Gatwick Express has been proposed for possible absorption by Southern as part of the DfT's Brighton Main Line Route Utilisation Strategy. This could take place before the expiry of the current Gatwick Express franchise.

[4] The new Greater Western franchise started on 1 April 2006 and incorporates the former Great Western, Wessex Trains and Thames Trains franchises. Awarded for seven years with a possible extension by a further three if performance targets are met.

[5] Incorporates the former Anglia and Great Eastern franchises and the West Anglia half of West Anglia Great Northern. Awarded for seven years with a likely extension for a further three.

[6] The new Integrated Kent franchise started on 1 April 2006 for an initial period of six years, to be extended by a further two if performance targets are met.

[7] The new East Coast franchise started on 1 May 2005 for an initial period of seven years, to be extended by a further three if performance targets are met.

[8] These two franchises will be combined to form the new South Western franchise on 3 February 2007, held by Stagecoach Holdings.

[9] Now under control of Merseytravel PTE instead of the DfT. Franchise due to be reviewed after seven years and then every five years to fit in with Merseyside Local Transport Plan.

[10] Due to be replaced by the new East Midlands franchise, incorporating all existing Midland Mainline and East Midlands area Central Trains services.

[11] Due to be abolished on expiry. Services to be split between a new London Rail franchise (control of which will be transferred to Transport for London) and the new West Midlands franchise.

[12] Urban and rural services previously run by Arriva Trains Northern and First North Western were transferred to the new Northern franchise on 12 December 2004. Trans-Pennine services formerly run by these operators were taken over by the new Trans-Pennine Express franchise on 1 February 2004. The Northern franchise runs for up to 8¾ years.

[13] Incorporates the former Thameslink franchise and Great Northern half of the former West Anglia Great Northern franchise. Runs for six years with a possible extension for up to three years depending on performance targets.

A major reorganisation of franchises is under way. See **Today's Railways UK** magazine for developments.

The following operators run non-franchised services only:

Operator	Trading Name	Route
BAA	Heathrow Express	London Paddington–Heathrow Airport
Hull Trains §	Hull Trains	London King's Cross–Hull
West Coast Railway	West Coast Railway Company	Birmingham–Stratford-on-Avon Fort William–Mallaig* York–Scarborough*

* Special summer-dated services only.
§ Owned by First Group.

INTERNATIONAL PASSENGER OPERATIONS

Eurostar (UK) operates international passenger-only services between the United Kingdom and continental Europe, jointly with French National Railways (SNCF) and Belgian National Railways (SNCB/NMBS). Eurostar (UK) is a subsidiary of London & Continental Railways, which is jointly owned by National Express Group plc and British Airways.

In addition, a service for the conveyance of accompanied road vehicles through the Channel Tunnel is provided by the tunnel operating company, Eurotunnel.

FREIGHT TRAIN OPERATIONS

The following operators operate freight train services under "Open Access" arrangements:

English Welsh & Scottish Railway Ltd (EWS).
Fastline.
Freightliner Ltd.
GB Railfreight Ltd. (owned by First Group)
Direct Rail Services Ltd.
FM Rail
Advenza (Cotswold Rail)

INTRODUCTION

SCOPE

This section contains details of all locomotives which can run on Britain's national railway network, plus those of Eurotunnel. Locomotives which are owned by, for example, EWS and Freightliner which have been withdrawn from service and awaiting disposal are listed in the main list, as are those owned by companies such as FM Rail, Harry Needle and DRS which are awaiting possible restoration to service. Only preserved locomotives which are currently used or are likely to be used on the national network in the foreseeable future are included. Others, which may be Network Rail registered but not at present certified for use, are not included, but will be found in the Platform 5 book, "Preserved locomotives and Multiple Units". Former BR locos classed as in industrial use (without Network Rail acceptance) in the UK are now listed in section 4 of this book. Locos already at scrapyards are not generally included, unless they are there for storage purposes and not for disposal.

LOCO CLASSES

Loco classes are listed in numerical order of class. Principal details and dimensions are quoted for each class in metric and/or imperial units as considered appropriate bearing in mind common UK usage.

All dimensions and weights are quoted for locomotives in an "as new" condition with all necessary supplies (e.g. oil, water and sand) on board. Dimensions are quoted in the order length x width. Lengths quoted are over buffers or couplers as appropriate. All widths quoted are maxima. Where two different wheel diameter dimensions are shown, the first refers to powered wheels and the second refers to non-powered wheels.

NUMERICAL LISTINGS

Locomotives are listed in numerical order. Where numbers actually carried are different from those officially allocated, these are noted in class headings where appropriate. Where locomotives have been recently renumbered, the most immediate previous number is shown in parentheses. Each locomotive entry is laid out as in the following example:

RSL No. Detail Livery Owner Pool   *Allocn.   Name*

47813 +m **CD**   CD   CRRH   MM   John Peel

Detail Differences. Only detail differences which currently affect the areas and types of train which locomotives may work are shown. All other detail differences are specifically excluded. Where such differences occur within a class or part class, they are shown in the "Detail" column alongside the individual locomotive number.

Standard abbreviations used are:

a	Train air brake equipment only.
b	Drophead buckeye couplers.
c	Scharfenberg couplers.
d	Fitted with retractable Dellner couplers.
k	Fitted with Swinghead Automatic "buckeye" combination couplers.
p	Train air, vacuum and electro-pneumatic brakes.
r	RETB fitted
s	Slow Speed Control equipment.
v	Train vacuum brake only.
x	Train air and vacuum brakes ("Dual brakes").
+	Additional fuel tank capacity.
§	Sandite laying equipment.

In all cases use of the above abbreviations indicates the equipment indicated is normally operable. Meaning of non-standard abbreviations and symbols is detailed in individual class headings.

Codes. Codes are used to denote the livery, owner, pool and depot of each locomotive. Details of these will be found in section 5 of this book.

Names. Only names carried with official sanction are listed. As far as possible names are shown in UPPER/lower case characters as actually shown on the name carried on the locomotive.

GENERAL INFORMATION

CLASSIFICATION AND NUMBERING

All locomotives are classified and allocated numbers by the Rolling Stock Library under the TOPS numbering system, introduced in 1972. This comprises a two-digit class number followed by a three-digit serial number. Where the actual number carried by a locomotive differs from the allocated number, or where an additional number is carried to the allocated number, this is shown by a note in the class heading.

For diesel locomotives, class numbers offer an indication of engine horsepower as shown in the table below.

Class No. Range	Engine h.p.
01–14	0–799
15–20	800–1000
21–31	1001–1499
32–39	1500–1999
40–54, 57	2000–2999
55–56, 58–69	3000+

For electric locomotives class numbers are allocated in ascending numerical order under the following scheme:

Class 70–80   direct current and DC/diesel dual system locomotives.
Class 81 onwards alternating current and AC/DC dual system locos.

Numbers in the 89xxx series are allocated by the Rolling Stock Library to locomotives which have been de-registered but subsequently re-registered for use on the Network Rail network and whose original number has already been re-used. 89xxx numbers are normally only carried inside locomotive cabs and are not carried externally in normal circumstances.

WHEEL ARRANGEMENT

For main line locomotives the number of driven axles on a bogie or frame is denoted by a letter (A = 1, B = 2, C = 3 etc.) and the number of non-powered axles is denoted by a number. The use of the letter "o" after a letter indicates each axle is individually powered, whilst the "+" symbol indicates bogies are inter-coupled.

For shunting locomotives, the Whyte notation is used. In this notation the number of leading wheels are given, followed by the number of driving wheels and then the trailing wheels.

HAULAGE CAPABILITY OF DIESEL LOCOMOTIVES

The haulage capability of a diesel locomotive depends upon three basic factors:

1. Adhesive weight. The greater the weight on the driving wheels, the greater the adhesion and more tractive power can be applied before wheelslip occurs.

2. The characteristics of its transmission. To start a train the locomotive has to exert a pull at standstill. A direct drive diesel engine cannot do this, hence the need for transmission. This may be mechanical, hydraulic or electric. The present British Standard for locomotives is electric transmission. Here the diesel engine drives a generator or alternator and the current produced is fed to the traction motors. The force produced by each driven wheel depends on the current in its traction motor. In other words, the larger the current, the harder it pulls. As the locomotive speed increases, the current in the traction motor falls, hence the *Maximum Tractive Effort* is the maximum force at its wheels the locomotive can exert at a standstill. The electrical equipment cannot take such high currents for long without overheating. Hence the *Continuous Tractive Effort* is quoted which represents the current which the equipment can take continuously.

3. The power of its engine. Not all power reaches the rail, as electrical machines are approximately 90% efficient. As the electrical energy passes through two such machines (the generator or alternator and the traction motors), the *Power at Rail* is approximately 81% (90% of 90%) of the engine power, less a further amount used for auxiliary equipment such as radiator fans, traction motor blowers, air compressors, battery charging, cab heating, Electric Train Supply (ETS) etc. The power of the locomotive is proportional to the tractive effort times the speed. Hence when on full power there is a speed corresponding to the continuous tractive effort.

HAULAGE CAPABILITY OF ELECTRIC LOCOMOTIVES

Unlike a diesel locomotive, an electric locomotive does not develop its power on board and its performance is determined only by two factors, namely its weight and the characteristics of its electrical equipment. Whereas a diesel locomotive tends to be a constant power machine, the power of an electric locomotive varies considerably. Up to a certain speed it can produce virtually a constant tractive effort. Hence power rises with speed according to the formula given in section three above, until a maximum speed is reached at which tractive effort falls, such that the power also falls. Hence the power at the speed corresponding to the maximum tractive effort is lower than the maximum speed.

BRAKE FORCE

The brake force is a measure of the braking power of a locomotive. This is shown on the locomotive data panels so operating staff can ensure sufficient brake power is available on freight trains.

ELECTRIC TRAIN SUPPLY (ETS)

A number of locomotives are equipped to provide a supply of electricity to the train being hauled to power auxiliaries such as heating, cooling fans, air conditioning and kitchen equipment. ETS is provided from the locomotive by means of a separate alternator (except Class 33 locos, which have a DC generator). The ETS index of a locomotive is a measure of the electrical power available for train supply.

Similarly, most loco-hauled coaches also have an ETS index, which in this case is a measure of the power required to operate equipment mounted in the coach. The sum of the ETS indices of all the hauled vehicles in a train must not exceed the ETS index of the locomotive.

ETS is commonly (but incorrectly) known as ETH (Electric Train Heating), which is a throwback to the days before loco-hauled coaches were equipped with electrically powered auxiliary equipment other than for train heating.

ROUTE AVAILABILITY (RA)

This is a measure of a railway vehicle's axle load. The higher the axle load of a vehicle, the higher the RA number on a scale from 1 to 10. Each Network Rail route has a RA number and in general no vehicle with a higher RA number may travel on that route without special clearance.

MULTIPLE & PUSH-PULL WORKING

Multiple working between vehicles (i.e. two or more powered vehicles being driven from one cab) is facilitated by jumper cables connecting the vehicles. However, not all types are compatible with each other, and a number of different systems are in use, each system being incompatible with any other.

Association of American Railroads (AAR) System: Classes 59, 66, and 67.
Blue Star Coupling Code: Classes 20, 25, 31, 33, and 37.
DRS System: Classes 20/3, 37 and 47.
Green Circle Coupling Code: Class 47 (not all equipped).
Orange Square Coupling Code: Class 50.
Red Diamond Coupling Code: Classes 56 and 58.
SR System: Classes 33/1, 73 and various electric multiple units.
Within Own Class only: Classes 43 and 60.

Many locomotives use a time-division multiplex (TDM) system for push-pull and multiple working which utilises the existing RCH jumper cables fitted to coaching stock vehicles. Previously these cables had only been used to control train lighting and public address systems.

Class 47 locos 47701–47717 were equipped with an older non-standard TDM system.

1. DIESEL LOCOMOTIVES

CLASS 08　　　BR/ENGLISH ELECTRIC　　　0-6-0

Built: 1955–1962 by BR at Crewe, Darlington, Derby Locomotive, Doncaster or Horwich Works.
Engine: English Electric 6KT of 298 kW (400 h.p.) at 680 r.p.m.
Main Generator: English Electric 801.
Traction Motors: Two English Electric 506.
Maximum Tractive Effort: 156 kN (35000 lbf).
Continuous Tractive Effort: 49 kN (11100 lbf) at 8.8 m.p.h.

Power At Rail: 194 kW (260 h.p.).	**Train Brakes:** Air & vacuum.
Brake Force: 19 t.	**Dimensions:** 8.92 x 2.59 m.
Weight: 49.6–50.4 t.	**Wheel Diameter:** 1372 mm.
Design Speed: 20 m.p.h.	**Maximum Speed:** 15 m.p.h.
Fuel Capacity: 3037 litres.	**RA:** 5.
Train Supply: Not equipped.	**Multiple Working:** Not equipped.

Notes: † – Equipped with remote control (Hima Sella system) for working at Celsa (formerly Allied Steel & Wire), Cardiff.

§ – Equipped with remote control (Cattron system) for evaluation purposes.

Non-standard liveries/numbering:

08350 Carries number D3420.
08414 As **DG**, but with BR & Railfreight Distribution logos and large bodyside numbers. Carries number D3529.
08442 Dark grey lower bodyside with light grey upper bodyside.
08460 Light grey with black underframe, cab doors, window surrounds & roof. Carries number D3575.
08480 Yellow with a red bodyside band. Carries number "TOTON No 1".
08499 Pullman Rail blue & white.
08527 White with a black roof & blue bodyside stripe.
08568 and 08730 Special Alstom (Springburn) livery. Dark grey lower bodyside with a light grey upper bodyside. Red solebar stripe.
08613 Blue with a white bodyside stripe & BOMBARDIER TRANSPORTATION branding.
08616 Carries number 3783.
08629 Red with italic numbers.
08648 Yellow with black cabsides & roof.
08649 Grey with blue, white & red stripes & Alstom logo. Carries number D3816.
08682 Dark blue with a grey roof.
08699 All-over mid blue.
08701 Carries number "Tyne 100".
08715 "Day-glo" orange.
08721 As **B**, but with a black roof & "Express parcels" branding with red & yellow stripe.
08824 Carries number "IEMD01".
08883 Caledonian Railway style blue.
08911 Royal blue with a grey roof.
08928 As **FO** with large bodyside numbers & light blue solebar.

Originally numbered in series D3000–D4192.

Class 08/0. Standard Design.

08077	**FL**	P	DFLS	FD	
08308 a	**CS**	RT	MOLO	IS	
08331	**GN**	RT	MOLS	ZB	
08350	**G**	LW	MBDL	CP	
08375 a	**RT**	RT	MOLO	TP	
08389 a	**E**	E	WSWM	BS	NOEL KIRTON OBE
08393 a	**E**	E	WSEM	TO	
08397 a	**E**	E	WZTS	AN	
08401 a	**DG**	E	WZTS	IM	
08402 a	**E**	E	WNXX	ML	
08405 a	**E**	E	WSWR	OC	
08410 a	**GL**	FG	HJXX	PZ	
08411 a	**B**	E	WNYX	AN	
08414 a	**O**	E	WNYX	TO	
08417 a	**SB**	SO	CDJD	ZA	
08418 a	**E**	E	WZTS	BS	
08428 a	**B**	E	WSEM	TO	
08441 a	**E**	E	WNYX	ML	
08442 a	**O**	E	WSXX	EH	RICHARD J. WENHAM EASTLEIGH DEPOT DECEMBER 1989–JULY 1999
08451	**GB**	VW	ATLO	WN	
08454	**SL**	VW	ATXX	WN	
08460 a	**O**	E	WZTS	AN	
08466 a†	**E**	E	WSAW	MG	
08472 a	**WA**	WA	RFSH	EC	
08480 a	**O**	E	WSXX	TO	
08482 a	**E**	E	WRLN	TD	
08483 a	**GL**	FG	HJXX	OO	DUSTY Driver David Miller
08485 a	**B**	E	WZTS	CU	
08489 a	**E**	E	WZTS	MH	
08492 a	**B**	HN	HNRS	BH	
08493 a	**B**	RT	MOLS	DW (S)	
08495	**E**	E	WSNE	TE	
08499 a	**O**	E	WSXX	CF	
08500	**E**	E	WSSC	ML	
08506 a	**B**	E	WNXX	OC	
08507 a	**HN**	HN	HNRL	CZ	
08509 a	**F**	E	WNYX	IM	
08510 a	**B**	E	WZTS	EH	
08511 a	**E**	E	WNYX	AY	
08512 a	**E**	E	WSEM	TO	
08514 a	**E**	E	WSNE	TE	
08516 a	**E**	E	WSXX	BK	
08523	**ML**	RT	MOLO	SB	
08525	**MA**	MA	HISL	NL	
08526	**E**	E	WNTS	MG	
08527	**O**	HN	HNRS	BH	
08528	**DG**	E	WNTS	BS	

08529	**B**	RT	MOLS	ZB	
08530	**FL**	P	DFLS	FD	
08531 a	**DG**	P	DFLS	FD	
08535	**DG**	RT	MOLS	CP	
08536	**B**	MA	HISE	DY (S)	
08538	**DG**	E	WRWM	BS	
08540	**E**	E	WNTR	TO	
08541	**DG**	HN	HNRS	OC	
08543	**DG**	E	WNYX	BS	
08561	**B**	E	WNXX	TD	
08567	**E**	E	WNYX	AN	
08568 a	**O**	AM	ARZH	ZH	St. Rollox
08569	**E**	E	WNYX	DR	
08571 a	**WA**	WA	HBSH	BN	
08573	**RT**	RT	MOLO	WR	
08575	**FL**	P	DFLS	FD	
08577	**E**	E	WNTR	BS	
08578	**E**	E	WSWM	BS	
08580	**E**	E	WNYX	BS	
08582 a	**DG**	E	WNYX	DR	
08585	**FL**	P	DFLS	FD	Vicky
08587	**E**	E	WNXX	MG	
08588	**RT**	RT	MOLO	CTRL Ripple Lane	
08593	**E**	E	WSWM	BS	
08596 a†	**WA**	WA	RFSH	ZB	
08597	**E**	E	WNTR	DR	
08599	**E**	E	WNTR	IM	
08605	**E**	E	WSSC	ML	
08611	**V**	VW	ATXX	MA	Downhill C.S.
08613	**O**	RT	KCSI	ZI	
08615	**WA**	WA	RFSH	EC	
08616	**GW**	MA	HGSS	TS	COOKIE
08617	**VP**	VW	ATXX	WB	
08623	**E**	E	WNTR	TD	
08624	**FL**	P	DFLS	FD	
08629	**O**	AM	ARZN	ZN	
08630	**E**	E	WSGW	MG	
08631	**N**	FM	SDFR	DF	EAGLE
08632	**E**	E	WSWM	BS	
08633	**E**	E	WSEM	TO	
08635	**B**	E	WNYX	TO	
08641	**GL**	FG	HJSL	LA	
08644	**GL**	FG	HJSL	LA	
08645	**GL**	FG	HJSL	LA	
08646	**F**	E	WNXX	TD	
08648	**O**	RT	MOLO	NW	
08649	**O**	AM	ARZN	ZN	G.H. Stratton
08651 a	**DG**	E	WNYX	BS	
08653	**E**	E	WRWM	BS	
08662	**E**	E	WSNE	TE	
08663 a	**GL**	FG	HJSL	PM	

08664	**E**	E	WSLS	OC	DON GATES 1952-2000
08665	**E**	E	WNYX	HM	
08669 a	**WA**	WA	RFSH	ZB	
08670 a	**E**	E	WNYX	ML	
08676	**E**	E	WSWR	OC	
08682	**0**	BT	KDSD	ZF	Lionheart
08683	**E**	E	WNXX	TO	
08685	**E**	E	WSNE	TE	
08689 a	**E**	E	WSWR	OC	
08690	**MA**	MA	HISE	NL	
08691	**FL**	WA	DFLS	FD	Terri
08694 a	**E**	E	WNXX	OC	
08695 a	**E**	E	WNYX	AY	
08696 a	**G**	VW	ATLO	MA	LONGSIGHT TMD
08697	**B**	MA	HISE	DY (S)	
08698 a	**E**	E	WNTS	ML	
08699	**0**	CD	CROL	AS	
08701 a	**RX**	E	WSXX	TY	
08703 a	**E**	E	WSEM	TO	
08706	**E**	E	WSWM	BS	
08709	**E**	E	WSWM	BS	MOLLY'S DAY
08711 k	**RX**	E	WSEM	TO	
08714	**E**	E	WRGW	MG	Cambridge
08715 v	**0**	E	WNXX	CU	
08720 a	**E**	E	WNYX	ML	
08721	**0**	VW	ATLO	MA	STARLET
08724	**WA**	WA	HBSH	NL	
08730	**0**	AM	ARZH	ZH	The Caley
08735	**E**	E	WSEM	TO	
08737 a	**E**	E	WSWM	BS	
08738	**E**	E	WNXX	MG	
08742	**RX**	E	WNXX	BS	
08745	**FE**	P	DHLT	SZ	
08750 a	**RT**	RT	MOLO	WR	
08752 †	**E**	E	WSAW	MG	
08754	**FL**	RT	MOLO	MY	
08756	**DG**	RT	MOLO	ZB	
08757	**RG**	E	WSWR	OC	
08762	**RT**	RT	MOLO	ZB	
08765	**E**	E	WSLS	OC	
08770 a	**DG**	E	WNTR	MG	
08775	**E**	E	WSWM	BS	
08776 a	**DG**	E	WNTR	TE	
08782 a†	**CU**	E	WRWM	BS	CASTLETON WORKS
08783	**E**	E	WRWM	BS	
08784	**E**	E	WSEM	TO	
08785 a	**FL**	P	DFLS	FD	
08786 a	**DG**	E	WSLN	TD	
08788	**RT**	RT	MOLO	IS	
08790	**B**	VW	ATLO	MA	M.A. Smith
08792	**F**	E	WNXX	BS	

08795	**GL**	FG	HJSE	LE	
08798	**E**	E	WSSC	ML	
08799 a	**E**	E	WSNE	TE	ANDY BOWER
08802	**RX**	E	WNTS	AN	
08804	**E**	E	WSWR	OC	
08805	**B**	MA	HGSS	SI	
08807	**BR**	E	WNYX	ML	
08809	**AR**	CD	CREL	AS (S)	
08810 a	**AR**	LW	MBDL	CP	
08813 a	**DG**	HN	HNRS	LM	
08818	**HN**	HN	HNRL	LM	Molly
08819	**DG**	RT	MOLS	DW	
08822	**GL**	FG	HJSE	PM	
08824 ak	**K**	E	WSXX	CE	
08827 a	**B**	HN	HNRS	LM	
08828 a	**E**	E	WSXX	BS	
08830	**LW**	AW	MBDL	ZB	
08834	**DR**	DR	XHSH	KM	
08836	**GL**	FG	HJXX	PM	
08842	**E**	E	WSSC	ML	
08844	**E**	E	WRWM	BS	CHRIS WREN 1955–2002
08847	**CD**	CD	CREL	NC	
08853 a	**B**	WA	RFSH	BN	
08854 †	**E**	E	WRLS	OC	
08856	**B**	E	WNXX	DC	
08865	**E**	E	WSWR	OC	
08866	**E**	E	WSSC	ML	
08868	**B**	HN	HNRL	CP	
08869	**G**	HN	HNRS	LM	
08871	**CD**	CD	CREL	NC	
08872	**E**	E	WZTS	TD	TONY LONG STRATFORD DEPOT 1971–2002
08874	**SL**	RT	MOLO	BY	Catherine
08877	**DG**	E	WSXX	SP	
08879	**E**	E	WSLS	OC	
08881	**DG**	E	WZTS	ML	
08883	**O**	E	WNYX	ML	
08884	**B**	E	WZTS	BS	
08885	**GB**	RT	MOLO	MY	
08886 §	**E**	E	WSAW	MG	
08887 a	**VP**	VW	ATLO	LL	
08888	**E**	E	WNTS	DR	
08890	**DG**	E	WNYX	EH	
08891	**FL**	P	DFLS	FD	J.R 1951–2005
08892	**DR**	DR	XHSH	KM	
08894	**B**	E	WNYX	AN	
08896	**E**	E	WNXX	TO	
08897	**E**	E	WSWM	BS	
08899	**MA**	MA	HISE	DY	
08900	**DG**	E	WNTS	MG	
08902	**B**	E	WNYX	AN	
08904	**E**	E	WSLN	TD	

08905		E	E	WNTS	BS	
08907		E	E	WRWM	BS	
08908		MM	MA	HISL	DY	
08909		E	E	WREM	TO	
08910		B	E	WNYX	TO	
08911		O	NM	MBDL	YK	
08912		B	E	WNYX	TO	
08913		E	E	WNXX	ML	
08915		F	E	WNXX	TO	
08918		DG	E	WNTS	OC	
08919		RX	E	WNYX	OC	
08920		F	E	WNXX	BS	
08921	†	E	E	WSAW	MG	
08922		DG	E	WRSC	ML	
08924		E	E	WNTS	ML	
08925		B	E	WNXX	DR	
08926		B	E	WNYX	AN	
08927		B	E	WNTS	ML	
08928		O	HN	HNRS	LM	
08933		E	E	WRLS	OC	
08934	a	VP	VW	ATLO	WB	
08936		HN	HN	CREL	WN	
08939		E	E	WRWR	OC	
08941		E	E	WSAW	MG	
08942		B	E	WNYX	TO	
08946		FE	E	WNYX	AN	
08947		B	E	WNXX	WY	
08948	c	EP	EU	GPSS	NP	
08950		MA	MA	HISL	NL	
08951	†	E	E	WNTS	AN	FRED
08953	a	DG	E	WNXX	DR	
08954		F	E	WNXX	AN	
08955		F	E	WNXX	BS	
08956		SB	SO	CDJD	ZA	

Class 08/9. Reduced height cab. Converted 1985–1987 by BR at Landore T&RSMD.

08993		E	E	WNTR	DR	ASHBURNHAM
08994	a	E	E	WSEM	TO	
08995	a	E	E	WNTR	MG	

▲ Freightliner-liveried 08691 "Terri" awaits its next turn of duty at Felixstowe North Terminal on 25/05/05. **Chris Booth**

▼ EWS-liveried 09022 shunts in Rugby Yard on 14/05/05. **Mark Beal**

DRS-liveried 20307 and 20309 are seen heading south on the West Coast Main Line at Red Bank with 6K73 15.38 Sellafield–Crewe Nuclear Flasks on 30/05/06.

Paul Senior

▲ Inter-City-liveried 31454 "HEART OF WESSEX" leads a 5Z33 09.42 Oxley–arrow Hill (via Derby) stock movement at Chesterfield on 06/07/06. 47145 was n the rear.
Robert Pritchard

▼ West Coast Railway Company-liveried 33207 "Jim Martin" found use at the o'ness & Kinneil diesel gala on 29/04/06. Here it is seen near Birkhill with an fternoon service from Bo'ness.
Ian Lothian

37612 and 37218 storm through Lichfield Trent Valley with 4L46 11.18 Ditton–Purfleet DRS Intermodal on 08/06/06.

BR Blue-liveried 40145 passes Diggle with a Pathfinder railtour from Crewe to Whitby on 03/06/06. **Gavin Morrison**

▲ Carrying the new First Group "Dynamic Lights" livery 43009 "First transforming travel" leads 43126 at Duffryn with an unidentified e.c.s. working to Cardiff Central on 20/05/06.   **John Catterson**

▼ A GNER HST set led by 43119 "Harrogate Spa" forms the 07.00 Edinburgh–London King's Cross at Eaton Lane Crossing near Retford on 14/07/06.
                                                                                        Andrew Wills

FM Rail's 47145 "MYRDDIN EMRYS" is seen working 6Z59 11.00 York North Yard–Coalville wagon movement at Milford, Derbyshire on 12/07/06.   **Mick Tindall**

Revised BR Blue-liveried 50049 "Defiance" passes Ponthir, just north of Newport, with 1Z47 16.20 Cardiff–Crewe

CLASS 09　　　BR/ENGLISH ELECTRIC　　　0-6-0

Built: 1959–1962 by BR at Darlington or Horwich Works.
Engine: English Electric 6KT of 298 kW (400 h.p.) at 680 r.p.m.
Main Generator: English Electric 801.
Traction Motors: English Electric 506.
Maximum Tractive Effort: 111 kN (25000 lbf).
Continuous Tractive Effort: 39 kN (8800 lbf) at 11.6 m.p.h.

Power At Rail: 201 kW (269 h.p.).	**Train Brakes:** Air & vacuum.
Brake Force: 19 t.	**Dimensions:** 8.92 x 2.59 m.
Weight: 49 t.	**Wheel Diameter:** 1372 mm.
Design Speed: 27 m.p.h.	**Maximum Speed:** 27 m.p.h.
Fuel Capacity: 3037 litres.	**RA:** 5.
Train Supply: Not equipped.	**Multiple Working:** Not equipped.

Class 09/0 were originally numbered D3665–D3671, D3719–3721, D4099–D4114.

Class 09/0. Built as Class 09.

09001		**E**	E	WSGW	MG
09003		**E**	E	WSWR	OC
09005	k	**E**	E	WRLS	OC
09006		**E**	E	WSLS	OC
09007		**ML**	E	WNTS	DR
09008		**E**	E	WNTR	BS
09009		**E**	E	WNXX	SL	Three Bridges C.E.D.
09010		**DG**	E	WNTR	HG
09011		**DG**	E	WNTS	MG
09012		**DG**	E	WNXX	HG
09013		**DG**	E	WSGW	MG
09014		**DG**	E	WSNE	TE
09015		**E**	E	WSGW	MG
09016		**E**	E	WNXX	BZ
09017		**E**	E	WSGW	MG
09018		**E**	E	WNXX	HG
09019		**ML**	E	WSWR	OC
09020		**E**	E	WSGW	MG
09021		**E**	E	WNXX	DR
09022	a	**E**	E	WSWM	BS
09023	a	**E**	E	WSEM	TO
09024		**ML**	E	WSLS	OC
09026		**G**	SN	HWSU	BI	Cedric Wares

Class 09/1. Converted from Class 08. 110 V electrical equipment.
Converted: 1992–1993 by RFS Industries, Kilnhurst.

09101	(08833)	**DG**	E	WSGW	MG
09102	(08832)	**DG**	E	WNTS	MG
09103	(08766)	**DG**	E	WSSC	ML
09104	(08749)	**DG**	E	WNXX	AN
09105	(08835)	**DG**	E	WSGW	MG
09106	(08759)	**DG**	E	WSEM	TO
09107	(08845)	**DG**	E	WRSC	ML

Class 09/2. Converted from Class 08. 90 V electrical equipment.
Converted: 1992 by RFS Industries, Kilnhurst.

09201	(08421)	ak	**DG**	E	WSNE	TE
09202	(08732)		**DG**	E	WNYX	DR
09203	(08781)		**DG**	E	WNYX	CE
09204	(08717)		**DG**	E	WNXX	TY
09205	(08620)		**DG**	E	WSNE	TE

CLASS 20   ENGLISH ELECTRIC   Bo-Bo

Built: 1957–1968 by English Electric Company at Vulcan Foundry, Newton le Willows or by Robert Stephenson & Hawthorn at Darlington.
Engine: English Electric 8SVT Mk. II of 746 kW (1000 h.p.) at 850 r.p.m.
Main Generator: English Electric 819/3C.
Traction Motors: English Electric 526/5D or 526/8D.
Maximum Tractive Effort: 187 kN (42000 lbf).
Continuous Tractive Effort: 111 kN (25000 lbf) at 11 m.p.h.

Power At Rail: 574 kW (770 h.p.).	**Train Brakes:** Air & vacuum.
Brake Force: 35 t.	**Dimensions:** 14.25 x 2.67 m.
Weight: 73.4–73.5 t.	**Wheel Diameter:** 1092 mm.
Design Speed: 75 m.p.h.	**Maximum Speed:** 75 m.p.h.
Fuel Capacity: 1727 litres.	**RA:** 5.
Train Supply: Not equipped.	**Multiple Working:** Blue Star.

Non-standard liveries/numbering:

20088 RFS grey.
20092 BR Central Services red & grey.
20132 Carries number D8132.
20138 and 20215 As **F0** but with a red solebar stripe.
20906 Carries no number.

Originally numbered in series D8007–D8190, D8315–D8325.

Class 20/0. Standard Design.

20016	**B**	HN	HNRS	LM
20032	**B**	HN	HNRS	LM
20057	**B**	HN	HNRS	LM
20066	**B**	HN	HNRL	BH
20072	**B**	HN	HNRS	LM
20081	**B**	HN	HNRS	LM
20088	**0**	HN	HNRS	LM
20092	**0**	HN	HNRS	BH
20096	**F**	HN	ADFL	BH
20121	**B**	HN	HNRS	BH
20132	**G**	HN	HNRS	BH
20138	**0**	HN	HNRS	LM
20215	**0**	HN	HNRS	LM

Class 20/3. Direct Rail Services refurbished locos. Details as Class 20/0 except:

Refurbished: 1995–1996 by Brush Traction at Loughborough (20301–20305) or 1997–1998 by RFS(E) at Doncaster (20306–20315). Disc indicators or headcode panels removed.

Train Brakes: Air.	**Maximum Speed:** 75 m.p.h.	
Weight: 76 t.	**Fuel Capacity:** 2900 (+ 4909) litres.	
Brake Force: 35 t.	**RA:** 6.	

Multiple Working: DRS system.

20301	(20047)	+	**DR**	DR XHNR	KM	Max Joule 1958–1999
20302	(20084)		**DR**	DR XHNR	KM	
20303	(20127)	+	**DR**	DR XHNR	KM	
20304	(20120)		**DR**	DR XHNR	KM	
20305	(20095)		**DR**	DR XHNR	KM	
20306	(20131)	+	**DR**	DR XHNR	KM	
20307	(20128)	+	**DR**	DR XHNR	KM	
20308	(20187)	+	**DR**	DR XHNR	KM	
20309	(20075)	+	**DR**	DR XHNR	KM	
20310	(20190)	+	**DR**	DR XHNR	KM	
20311	(20102)	+	**DR**	DR XHNR	KM	
20312	(20042)	+	**DR**	DR XHNR	KM	
20313	(20194)	+	**DR**	DR XHNC	KM	
20314	(20117)	+	**DR**	DR XHNR	KM	
20315	(20104)	+	**DR**	DR XHMW	ZH	

Class 20/9. Harry Needle Railroad Company (former Hunslet-Barclay/DRS) locos.
Details as Class 20/0 except:

Refurbished: 1989 by Hunslet-Barclay at Kilmarnock.
Train Brakes: Air.   **Fuel Capacity:** 1727 (+ 4727) litres.

20901	(20101)		**DR**	HN HNRL		Flixborough Wharf
20902	(20060)	+	**DR**	HN HNRS	LM	
20903	(20083)	+	**DR**	HN HNRS	ZH	
20904	(20041)		**DR**	HN HNRS	BH	
20905	(20225)	+	**F**	HN XHNR	BH	
20906	(20219)		**DR**	HN HNRS	CP	

CLASS 31 BRUSH/ENGLISH ELECTRIC A1A-A1A

Built: 1958–1962 by Brush Traction at Loughborough.
Engine: English Electric 12SVT of 1100 kW (1470 h.p.) at 850 r.p.m.
Main Generator: Brush TG160-48.   **Traction Motors:** Brush TM73-68.
Maximum Tractive Effort: 160 kN (35900 lbf).
Continuous Tractive Effort: 83 kN (18700 lbf) at 23.5 m.p.h.
Power At Rail: 872 kW (1170 h.p.).   **Train Brakes:** Air & vacuum.
Brake Force: 49 t.   **Dimensions:** 17.30 x 2.67 m.
Weight: 106.7–111 t.   **Wheel Diameter:** 1092/1003 mm.
Design Speed: 90 m.p.h.   **Maximum Speed:** 90 m.p.h.
Fuel Capacity: 2409 (+ 4820) litres. **RA:** 5 or 6.
Train Supply: Not equipped.   **Multiple Working:** Blue Star.

Originally numbered D5520–D5699, D5800–D5862 (not in order).

Non-standard livery:

31301 As **F0** but with a red solebar stripe.

Class 31/1. Standard Design. RA: 5.

31102	**CE**	NR	QETS	TH
31105	**Y**	NR	QADD	DF
31106	**FR**	HJ	SDPP	DF	SPALDING TOWN
31107	**K**	NR	QETS	DF
31128	**FR**	FM	SDPP	DF	CHARYBDIS
31190	**WS**	FM	SDFR	DF	GRYPHON
31200	**F**	NR	QETS	TH
31233 a	**Y**	NR	QADD	DF
31285	**Y**	NR	QADD	DF
31301	**0**	FM	SDXL	MQ
31308	**CE**	HN	HNRS	OC
31319	**F**	NR	QETS	TH

Class 31/4. Electric Train Supply equipment. RA: 6.
Train Supply: Electric, index 66.

31415	**B**	FM	SDXL	MQ
31420	**IM**	E	WNXX	OC
31422	**IM**	FM	SDXL	TM
31423	**IM**	FM	SDXL	MQ
31427	**B**	E	WNXX	OC
31437	**CE**	FM	SDXL	MQ
31439	**RR**	FM	SDXL	MQ
31452	**FR**	FM	SDPP	DF	MINOTAUR
31454	**IC**	FM	SDPP	DF	THE HEART OF WESSEX
31459	**FM**	FM	SDPP	DF	CERBERUS
31460	**B**	FM	SDXL	BH
31461 +	**DG**	FM	SDXL	DF
31466 a	**E**	E	WNXX	OC
31468	**FR**	FM	SDPP	DF	HYDRA

Class 31/6. ETS through wiring and controls. RA: 5.

31601	(31186)	**WX**	FM	SDPP	DF	GAUGE 'O' GUILD 1956–2006
31602	(31191)	**FR**	FM	SDPP	DF	CHIMAERA

CLASS 33   BRCW/SULZER   Bo-Bo

Built: 1960–1962 by the Birmingham Railway Carriage & Wagon Company at Smethwick.
Engine: Sulzer 8LDA28 of 1160 kW (1550 h.p.) at 750 r.p.m.
Main Generator: Crompton Parkinson CG391B1.
Traction Motors: Crompton Parkinson C171C2.
Maximum Tractive Effort: 200 kN (45000 lbf).
Continuous Tractive Effort: 116 kN (26000 lbf) at 17.5 m.p.h.
Power At Rail: 906 kW (1215 h.p.). **Train Brakes:** Air & vacuum.
Brake Force: 35 t. **Dimensions:** 15.47 x 2.82 (2.64 m. 33/2).
Weight: 76 t. **Wheel Diameter:** 1092 mm.
Design Speed: 85 m.p.h. **Maximum Speed:** 85 m.p.h.
Fuel Capacity: 3410 litres. **RA:** 6.
Train Supply: Electric, index 48 (750 V DC only).
Multiple Working: Blue Star.

Originally numbered in series D6500–D6597 but not in order.

Non-standard liveries/numbering:

33046 All over mid-blue. Carries no number.
33109 Carries number D6525.

Class 33/0. Standard Design.

33021	**FR**	FM	SDFR	DF (S)	Eastleigh
33025	**WS**	WC	MBDL	CS	Glen Falloch
33029	**WS**	WC	MBDL	CS	Glen Loy
33030	**DR**	WC	MBDL	CS (S)	
33046	**O**	FM	SDXL	DF	

Class 33/1. Fitted with Buckeye Couplings & SR Multiple Working Equipment for use with SR EMUs, TC stock & Class 73s. Also fitted with flashing light adaptor for use on Weymouth Quay line.

33103 b	**FR**	CM	SDFR	DF	SWORDFISH
33109 b	**B**	FM	SDXL	CP	

Class 33/2. Built to former Loading Gauge of Tonbridge–Battle Line.
All equipped with slow speed control.

33202	**FR**	FM	SDFR	DF	METEOR
33207	**WS**	WC	MBDL	CS	Jim Martin

CLASS 37   ENGLISH ELECTRIC   Co-Co

Built: 1960–1965 by English Electric Company at Vulcan Foundry, Newton le Willows or by Robert Stephenson & Hawthorn at Darlington.
Engine: English Electric 12CSVT of 1300 kW (1750 h.p.) at 850 r.p.m.
Main Generator: English Electric 822/10G.
Traction Motors: English Electric 538/A.
Maximum Tractive Effort: 245 kN (55500 lbf).
Continuous Tractive Effort: 156 kN (35000 lbf) at 13.6 m.p.h.
Power At Rail: 932 kW (1250 h.p.).   **Train Brakes:** Air & vacuum.
Brake Force: 50 t.   **Dimensions:** 18.75 x 2.74 m.
Weight: 102.8–108.4 t.   **Wheel Diameter:** 1092 mm.
Design Speed: 90 m.p.h.   **Maximum Speed:** 80 m.p.h.
Fuel Capacity: 4046 (+ 7678) litres.   **RA:** 5 (§ 6).
Train Supply: Not equipped.
Multiple Working: Blue Star († DRS system).

Originally numbered D6600–D6608, D6700–D6999 (not in order).

Non-standard liveries/numbering:

37351 Carries number 37002 on one side only.
37402 Light grey lower bodyside & dark grey upper bodyside.
37403 Also carries number D6607.
37411 Also carries number D6990.

Class 37/0. Standard Design. Details as above.

37010	a	**CE**	HN	HNRS	LM
37023		**ML**	DR	XHSS	LB
37029	§	**DR**	DR	XHNR	KM
37038	†	**DR**	DR	XHNR	KM
37042	+	**E**	E	WNTR	DR
37046	a	**CE**	E	WZKF	TY
37047	+	**ML**	E	WNTA	HG
37051		**E**	DR	XHSS	LB
37055	+	**ML**	E	WNXX	TE
37057	+	**E**	E	WNTA	HM
37058	a+	**CE**	E	WZKF	TY
37059	a+†	**DR**	DR	XHNR	KM
37065	+	**ML**	E	WNTR	TT
37069	a+†	**DR**	DR	XHNR	KM
37077	a	**ML**	E	WZKF	BK
37087	a	**DR**	DR	XHNR	KM
37100	a	**F**	HN	HNRS	BH
37108	+	**WS**	TT	TTTC	CS (S)
37109		**E**	E	WNTA	HG
37114	r+	**E**	E	WNTA	BS	City of Worcester
37116	+	**B**	E	WNYX	EH
37146	a	**CE**	E	WNXX	TY
37158		**WS**	WC	MBDL	CS (S)
37165	a+	**CE**	PO	MBDL	CS (S)
37170	a	**CE**	HN	HNRS	LM

37174	a	**E**	E	WNTS	BS	
37178	+	**F**	HN	HNRS	BH	
37194		**DR**	DR	XHNR	KM	
37196	a	**CE**	E	WZKF	TY	
37197		**DR**	DR	XHNC	KM	
37203		**ML**	E	WNTR	BS	
37214		**WS**	WC	MBDL	CS	Loch Laidon
37216	+	**ML**	E	WNTR	ML	
37217	+	**B**	HN	HNRS	AY	
37218	†	**DR**	DR	XHNR	KM	
37220	+	**F**	HN	HNRS	LM	
37221	a	**F**	E	WZKF	TY	
37222		**F**	HN	HNRS	CS	
37229	§	**DR**	DR	XHNR	KM	Jonty Jarvis 8-12-1998 to 18-3-2005
37235		**F**	WC	MBDL	CS (S)	
37238	a+	**F**	E	WZKF	TY	
37248	+	**WS**	TT	MBDL	CS	Loch Arkaig
37250	a+	**F**	E	WZKF	TY	
37259	†	**DR**	DR	XHNR	KM	
37261	a+	**DR**	DR	XHNR	KM	
37293	a+	**ML**	E	WZKF	TY	
37294	a+	**CE**	E	WNXX	CD	
37308	+	**B**	E	WNTR	TT	

Class 37/3. Re-geared (CP7) bogies. Details as Class 37/0 except:

Maximum Tractive Effort: 250 kN (56180 lbf).
Continuous Tractive Effort: 184 kN (41250 lbf) at 11.4 m.p.h.
Design Speed: 80 m.p.h.

37351	+	**CE**	E	WNXX	CD	
37372		**ML**	E	WNTA	ML	
37375	a+	**ML**	E	WNTS	TO	
37377	+	**U**	E	WZKF	BK	
37379	a	**ML**	E	WNXX	BK	
37383	+	**ML**	RV	RTLS	CP	

Class 37/4. Refurbished with electric train supply equipment. Main generator replaced by alternator. Re-geared (CP7) bogies. Details as Class 37/0 except:
Main Alternator: Brush BA1005A.   **Power At Rail:** 935 kW (1254 h.p.).
Traction Motors: English Electric 538/5A.
Maximum Tractive Effort: 256 kN (57440 lbf).
Continuous Tractive Effort: 184 kN (41250 lbf) at 11.4 m.p.h.
Weight: 107 t.
Design Speed: 80 m.p.h.
Fuel Capacity: 7678 litres.
Train Supply: Electric, index 30.

37401	r	**GS**	E	WNTR	ML	
37402		**O**	E	WNTR	TO	Bont Y Bermo
37403	a	**G**	E	WNYX	MG	
37405	r	**E**	E	WKBM	ML	
37406	r	**E**	E	WKBM	ML	The Saltire Society

37407	F	E	WNYX	MO	
37408	E	E	WNYX	TO	
37409	F	E	WNXX	ML	
37410	E	E	WNTA	TE	
37411	G	E	WNTS	MG	CAERPHILLY CASTLE/CASTELL CAERFFILI
37412	F	E	WNXX	MG	Driver John Elliott
37413	E	E	WNXX	MG	
37415	E	E	WNXX	MG	
37416	GS	E	WNTS	ML	
37417 ra	E	E	WKBM	ML	Richard Trevithick
37418 r	E	E	WNTR	TT	
37419	E	E	WNTR	OC	
37420	RR	E	WNXX	CD	
37421 r	E	E	WNTR	ML	
37422	E	E	WNTR	EH	Cardiff Canton
37423	F	DR	XHSS	LB	
37424	F	E	WNYX	ML	
37425	BL	E	WKCK	MG	Pride of the Valleys/
					Balchder y Cymoedd
37426	E	E	WNXX	CD	
37427 r	E	E	WNTR	ML	
37428	GS	E	WNXX	MG	
37429	RR	E	WNXX	TT	
37430 a	F	E	WNYX	ML	

**Class 37/5. Refurbished without train supply equipment. Main generator
replaced by alternator. Re-geared (CP7) bogies.** Details as Class 37/4 except:
Maximum Tractive Effort: 248 kN (55590 lbf).
Weight: 106.1–110.0 t.

37503 r§	E	E	WNTA	DR	
37505 a§	F	E	WZKF	AY	British Steel Workington
37510 a	DR	DR	XHNR	KM	
37513 as§LH		E	WNXX	OC	
37515 as	DR	DR	XHNC	KM	
37516 s§	LH	E	WNTA	DR	
37517 as§LH		E	WNTA	HM	
37518 a§	F	E	WZKF	AY	
37519	F	E	WZKF	EH	
37520 r§	E	E	WNXX	CD	
37521 r§	E	E	WNTA	DR	English China Clays

**Class 37/6. Originally refurbished for Nightstar services. Main generator
replaced by alternator. UIC jumpers.** Details as Class 37/5 except:
Maximum Speed: 90 m.p.h.   **Train Brake:** Air.
Train Supply: Not equipped, but electric through wired.
Multiple Working: Blue Star († DRS system).

37601	EP	EU	GPSV	NP	
37602 †	DR	DR	XHNC	KM	
37603	EP	EU	GPSV	NP	
37604	EP	EU	GPSV	NP	
37605 †	DR	DR	XHNC	KM	

37606 †	**DR**	DR	XHNC	KM	
37607 †	**DR**	DR	XHNC	KM	
37608 †	**DR**	DR	XHNC	KM	
37609 †	**DR**	DR	XHNC	KM	
37610 †	**DR**	DR	XHNC	KM	The MALCOLM Group
37611 †	**DR**	DR	XHNC	KM	
37612 †	**DR**	DR	XHNC	KM	

Class 37/5 continued.

37667 rs§	**E**	HN	HNRS	BH	
37668 s§	**E**	E	WNTA	HM	
37669 r	**E**	E	WNTR	MG	
37670 r	**E**	E	WNTR	MG	St. Blazey T&RS Depot
37671 a	**F**	E	WZKF	TY	
37672 as	**F**	HN	HNRS	BH	
37673 §	**F**	E	WNXX	TE	
37674 §	**F**	E	WNTA	ML	Saint Blaise Church 1445–1995
37675 as§	**F**	E	WNTA	MG	Margam TMD
37676 a§	**F**	E	WNTA	HM	
37677 a§	**F**	E	WNXX	IM	
37678 a§	**F**	E	WNXX	BS	
37679 a§	**F**	E	WZKF	AY	
37680 a§	**F**	HN	HNRS	Hope	
37682 r§	**E**	E	WNTA	HM	
37683 a	**F**	E	WNXX	TE	
37684 ar§	**E**	E	WNTA	MG	Peak National Park
37685 a§	**IC**	E	WNTA	HM	
37688 §	**DR**	DR	XHSS	LB	
37689 a§	**F**	E	WNTA	HM	
37692 s§	**F**	E	WNTA	MG	Didcot Depot
37693 as	**F**	E	WZKF	TY	
37694 §	**E**	E	WNTR	TD	
37695 s§	**E**	E	WNTR	HM	
37696 as	**F**	E	WZKF	BK	
37698 a§	**LH**	E	WNTA	MG	

Class 37/7. Refurbished locos. Main generator replaced by alternator. Re-geared (CP7) bogies. Ballast weights added. Details as Class 37/5 except:
Main Alternator: GEC G564AZ (37796–803) Brush BA1005A (others).
Maximum Tractive Effort: 276 kN (62000 lbf).
Weight: 120 t.   **RA:** 7.

37701 as	**F**	E	WZKF	OC	
37702 s	**GIF**	E	WZKS	ES	
37703	**GIF**	E	WZKS	ES	
37704 s	**E**	HN	HNRS	MG	
37705	**F**	E	WZKF	ML	
37706	**E**	E	WNTA	HM	
37707	**E**	E	WNTA	BS	
37708 a	**F**	E	WNXX	HM	
37709	**F**	E	WNTA	MH	
37710	**LH**	E	WNTA	HM	

37712	a	**E**	E	WNTA	HM	
37713		**LH**	HN	HNRS	CD	
37714	a	**GIF**	E	WZKS	ES	
37716		**GIF**	E	WZKS	ES	
37717		**E**	E	WNTA	HM	
37718		**GIF**	E	WZKS	ES	
37719	a	**F**	E	WZKF	OC	
37796	as	**F**	E	WZKF	TY	
37798		**ML**	E	WNTA	MG	
37799	as	**GIF**	E	WZKS	ES	
37800	a	**GIF**	E	WZKS	ES	
37801	s	**GIF**	E	WZKS	ES	
37803	a	**ML**	E	WNXX	TY	
37883		**GIF**	E	WZKS	ES	
37884		**GIF**	E	WZKS	ES	
37886		**E**	E	WNTA	MH	Sir Dyfed/County of Dyfed
37887	s	**F**	E	WZKF	IM	
37888		**GIF**	E	WZKS	ES	
37890	a	**F**	E	WNTA	MG	
37891	a	**F**	E	WZKF	TY	
37892		**F**	E	WZKF	OC	Ripple Lane
37893		**E**	E	WNTA	BS	
37894	as	**F**	E	WZKF	TY	
37895	s	**E**	E	WNTA	BS	
37896	s	**F**	E	WNTA	MG	
37897	s	**F**	HN	HNRS	BS	
37898	s	**F**	HN	HNRS	MG	

CLASS 40   ENGLISH ELECTRIC   1Co-Co1

Built: 1958–1962 by the English Electric Co. at Vulcan Foundry, Newton le Willows.
Engine: English Electric 16SVT Mk2 of 1490 kW (2000 h.p.) at 850 r.p.m.
Main Generator: English Electric 822/4C.
Traction Motors: English Electric 526/5D or EE526/7D.
Maximum Tractive Effort: 231 kN (52000 lbf).
Continuous Tractive Effort: 137 kN (30900 lbf) at 18.8 m.p.h.

Power At Rail: 1160 kW (1550 h.p.).	**Train Brakes:** Air & vacuum.
Brake Force: 51 t.	**Dimensions:** 21.18 x 2.78 m.
Weight: 132 t.	**Wheel Diameter:** 914/1143 mm.
Design Speed: 90 m.p.h.	**Maximum Speed:** 90 m.p.h.
Fuel Capacity: 3250 litres.	**RA:** 6.
Train Supply: Steam.	**Multiple Working:** Not equipped.

| 40145 | **B** | 40 | ELRD | BQ |

CLASS 43   BREL/PAXMAN   Bo-Bo

Built: 1976–1982 by BREL at Crewe Works.
Engine: Paxman Valenta 12RP200L of 1680 kW (2250 h.p.) at 1500 r.p.m.
(* Paxman 12VP185 of 1565 kW (2100 h.p.) at 1500 r.p.m.).
(ø MTU 16V4000 R41R of 1680kW (2250 h.p.) at 1500 r.p.m.). Experimentally fitted by Angel Trains to two power cars in 2005 and now to be fitted to the entire First Great Western and GNER fleets.
Main Alternator: Brush BA1001B.
Traction Motors: Brush TMH68–46 or GEC G417AZ, frame mounted.
Maximum Tractive Effort: 80 kN (17980 lbf).
Continuous Tractive Effort: 46 kN (10340 lbf) at 64.5 m.p.h.
Power At Rail: 1320 kW (1770 h.p.).   **Train Brakes:** Air.
Brake Force: 35 t.   **Dimensions:** 17.79 x 2.71 m.
Weight: 70.25 t.   **Wheel Diameter:** 1020 mm.
Design Speed: 125 m.p.h.   **Maximum Speed:** 125 m.p.h.
Fuel Capacity: 4500 litres.   **RA:** 5.
Train Supply: Three-phase electric.
Multiple Working: Within class, jumpers at non-driving end only.

Notes: † Buffer fitted.

43013, 43014 and 43062 are fitted with measuring apparatus & front-end cameras.

Non-standard livery: 43101 All over black with a red cab.

Advertising livery: 43087 Hornby red with yellow decals.

43002	**FG**	A	IWRP	PM	TECHNIQUEST
43003	**FG**	A	IWRP	PM	ISAMBARD KINGDOM BRUNEL
43004 ø	**FH**	A	IWRP	PM	First for the future/
					First ar gyfer y dyfodol
43005	**FG**	A	IWRP	PM	
43006	**GN**	A	IECP	EC	Kingdom of Fife
43007	**MN**	A	IMLP	NL	
43008	**GN**	A	IECP	EC	
43009 ø	**FD**	A	IWRP	PM	First transforming travel
43010	**FG**	A	IWRP	PM	
43012	**FG**	A	IWRP	PM	
43013 †	**Y**	P	QCAR	EC	
43014 †	**Y**	P	QCAR	EC	
43015	**FG**	A	IWRP	PM	
43016	**FG**	A	IWRP	LE	Peninsula Medical School
43017	**FG**	A	IWRP	LE	
43018	**FG**	A	IWRP	LE	The Red Cross
43020	**FG**	A	IWRP	LA	John Grooms
43021	**FG**	A	IWRP	LA	
43022	**FG**	A	IWRP	PM	
43023	**FG**	A	IWRP	PM	County of Cornwall
43024	**FG**	A	IWRP	PM	
43025	**FG**	A	IWRP	PM	Exeter
43026	**FG**	A	IWRP	PM	City of Westminster
43027	**FG**	A	IWRP	PM	Glorious Devon

43028	**FG**	A	IWRP	PM	
43029	**FG**	A	IWRP	PM	
43030	**FG**	A	IWRP	PM	Christian Lewis Trust
43031	**FG**	A	IWRP	PM	
43032	**FG**	A	IWRP	PM	The Royal Regiment of Wales
43033	**FG**	A	IWRP	PM	Driver Brian Cooper
					15 June 1947–5 October 1999
43034	**FG**	A	IWRP	PM	The Black Horse
43035	**FG**	A	IWRP	PM	
43036	**FG**	A	IWRP	PM	
43037	**FG**	A	IWRP	PM	PENYDARREN
43038	**GN**	A	IECP	EC	City of Dundee
43039	**GN**	A	IECP	EC	
43040	**FG**	A	IWRP	PM	Bristol St. Philip's Marsh
43041	**FG**	A	IWRP	PM	City of Discovery
43042	**FG**	A	IWRP	PM	
43043 *	**MN**	P	IMLP	NL	
43044 *	**MN**	P	IMLP	NL	
43045 *	**MN**	P	IMLP	NL	
43046	**MN**	P	IMLP	NL	
43047 *	**MN**	P	IMLP	NL	
43048 *	**MN**	P	IMLP	NL	
43049 *	**MN**	P	IMLP	NL	Neville Hill
43050 *	**MN**	P	IMLP	NL	
43051	**MN**	P	IMLP	NL	
43052 *	**MN**	P	IMLP	NL	
43053	**MN**	P	IMLP	NL	
43054	**MN**	P	IMLP	NL	
43055 *	**MN**	P	IMLP	NL	
43056	**MN**	P	IMLP	NL	
43057	**MN**	P	IMLP	NL	
43058	**MN**	P	IMLP	NL	
43059 *	**MN**	P	IMLP	NL	
43060 *	**MN**	P	IMLP	NL	
43061 *	**MN**	P	IMLP	NL	
43062	**Y**	P	QCAR	EC	
43063	**FG**	P	IWRP	LA	
43064	**MN**	P	IMLP	NL	
43065 †	**V**	P	SBXL	LM	
43066	**MN**	P	IMLP	NL	
43067 †	**Y**	P	SBXL	LM	
43068 †	**V**	P	SBXL	LM	
43069	**MN**	P	IWRP	LA (S)	Rio Enterprise
43070	**CD**	P	IWRP	LA (S)	
43071	**FG**	P	IWRP	LA	
43072 *	**MN**	P	IMLP	NL	Derby Etches Park
43073 *	**MN**	P	IMLP	NL	
43074 *	**MN**	P	IMLP	NL	
43075 *	**MN**	P	IMLP	NL	
43076 *	**MN**	P	IMLP	NL	
43077	**MN**	P	IMLP	NL	

43078		**GN**	P	IWRP	LB (S)	
43079		**FG**	P	IWRP	LA	
43080	†	**GN**	P	SBXL	LM	
43081		**MN**	P	IMLP	NL	
43082	*	**MN**	P	IMLP	NL	
43083		**MN**	P	IMLP	NL	
43084	†	**V**	P	SBXL	LM	
43085		**MN**	P	IMLP	NL	
43086		**MN**	P	IWRP	LA (S)	
43087		**AL**	P	IWRP	LA (S)	
43088		**FG**	P	IWRP	LA	
43089		**Y**	P	QCAR	LB (S)	
43090		**V**	P	IECP	LB (S)	
43091		**FG**	P	IWRP	LA	
43092	ø	**FH**	FG	IWRP	LE	
43093	ø	**FH**	FG	IWRP	LE	
43094	ø	**FH**	FG	IWRP	LE	
43095		**GN**	A	IECP	EC	
43096		**GN**	A	IECP	EC	Stirling Castle
43097	ø	**FH**	FG	IWRP	LE	Environment Agency
43098	ø	**FH**	FG	IWRP	LE	
43099		**GN**	P	IECP	EC	Diocese of Newcastle
43100		**V**	P	IECP	LB (S)	
43101		**O**	P	SBXL	LB	
43102		**GN**	P	IECP	EC	
43103		**V**	P	SBXL	LM	
43104		**MN**	A	IMLP	NL	
43105		**GN**	A	IECP	EC	City of Inverness
43106		**GN**	A	IECP	EC	Fountains Abbey
43107		**GN**	A	IECP	EC	Tayside
43108		**GN**	A	IECP	EC	Old Course St Andrews
43109		**GN**	A	IECP	EC	Leeds International Film Festival
43110		**GN**	A	IECP	EC	Stirlingshire
43111		**GN**	A	IECP	EC	Scone Palace
43112		**GN**	A	IECP	EC	Doncaster
43113		**GN**	A	IECP	EC	The Highlands
43114		**GN**	A	IECP	EC	East Riding of Yorkshire
43115		**GN**	A	IECP	EC	Aberdeenshire
43116		**GN**	A	IECP	EC	The Black Dyke Band
43117		**GN**	A	IECP	EC	Bonnie Prince Charlie
43118		**GN**	A	IECP	EC	City of Kingston upon Hull
43119		**GN**	A	IECP	EC	Harrogate Spa
43120		**GN**	A	IECP	EC	National Galleries of Scotland
43121		**V**	P	SBXL	LM	
43122		**V**	FG	IWRP	LB (S)	
43123	†	**V**	P	SBXL	LM	
43124		**FG**	A	IWRP	LE	
43125		**FG**	A	IWRP	LE	Merchant Venturer
43126		**FG**	A	IWRP	LE	City of Bristol
43127		**FG**	A	IWRP	LE	Sir Peter Parker 1924–2002
						Cotswold Line 150

43128	**FG**	A	IWRP	LE	
43129	**FG**	A	IWRP	LE	
43130	**FG**	A	IWRP	LE	Sulis Minerva
43131	**FG**	A	IWRP	LE	Sir Felix Pole
43132	**FG**	A	IWRP	LE	
43133 ø	**FH**	A	IWRP	LE	
43134	**FG**	A	IWRP	LE	County of Somerset
43135	**FG**	A	IWRP	LE	QUAKER ENTERPRISE
43136	**FG**	A	IWRP	LE	
43137	**FG**	A	IWRP	LE	Newton Abbot 150
43138	**FG**	A	IWRP	LE	
43139	**FG**	A	IWRP	LE	Driver Stan Martin
					25 June 1960 – 6 November 2004
43140	**FG**	A	IWRP	LE	
43141	**FG**	A	IWRP	LE	
43142	**FG**	A	IWRP	LE	
43143	**FG**	A	IWRP	LE	Stroud 700
43144	**FG**	A	IWRP	LE	
43145	**FG**	A	IWRP	LE	
43146	**FG**	A	IWRP	LE	
43147	**FG**	A	IWRP	LE	
43148	**FG**	A	IWRP	LE	
43149	**FG**	A	IWRP	LE	BBC Wales Today
43150	**FG**	A	IWRP	LE	Bristol Evening Post
43151	**FG**	A	IWRP	LE	
43152	**FG**	A	IWRP	LE	
43153	**V**	FG	IWRP	LB (S)	
43154	**Y**	FG	IWRP	LB (S)	
43155 ø	**FH**	FG	IWRP	LE	
43156	**FG**	P	IWRP	LA	
43157	**V**	P	SBXL	LM	
43158 ø	**FH**	FG	IWRP	LE	
43159	**MN**	P	IWRP	LA (S)	
43160	**V**	P	QCAR	LB (S)	
43161	**FG**	P	IWRP	LA	
43162	**FG**	P	IWRP	LA	
43163	**FG**	A	IWRP	LA	
43164	**FG**	A	IWRP	LA	
43165 ø	**FH**	A	IWRP	LA	Prince Michael of Kent
43166	**MN**	A	IMLP	NL	
43167	**GN**	A	IECP	EC	DELTIC 50 1955–2005
43168 *	**FG**	A	IWRP	LA	
43169 *	**FG**	A	IWRP	LA	THE NATIONAL TRUST
43170 *	**FG**	A	IWRP	LA	Edward Paxman
43171	**FG**	A	IWRP	LA	
43172	**FG**	A	IWRP	LA	
43174	**FG**	A	IWRP	LA	Bristol–Bordeaux
43175 ø	**FH**	A	IWRP	LE	
43176	**FG**	A	IWRP	LA	
43177 *	**FG**	A	IWRP	LA	University of Exeter
43178	**MN**	A	IMLP	NL	

43179	*	**FG**	A	IWRP	LA	Pride of Laira
43180		**FG**	P	IWRP	LA	
43181		**FG**	A	IWRP	LA	Devonport Royal Dockyard 1693–1993
43182		**FG**	A	IWRP	LA	
43183		**FG**	A	IWRP	LA	
43184		**MN**	A	IMLP	NL	
43185		**FG**	A	IWRP	LA	Great Western
43186		**FG**	A	IWRP	LA	Sir Francis Drake
43187		**FG**	A	IWRP	LA	
43188		**FG**	A	IWRP	LA	City of Plymouth
43189		**FG**	A	IWRP	LA	RAILWAY HERITAGE TRUST
43190		**FG**	A	IWRP	LA	
43191	*	**FG**	A	IWRP	LA	Seahawk
43192		**FG**	A	IWRP	LA	City of Truro
43193		**MN**	P	IWRP	LA (S)	
43194		**V**	FG	IWRP	LB (S)	
43195		**FG**	P	IWRP	LA	
43196		**Y**	P	QCAR	EC	
43197		**GN**	P	IWRP	LB (S)	
43198	ø	**FH**	FG	IWRP	LE	

Class 43/2. Proposed numbering series for GNER power cars when rebuilt with new MTU engines. It is planned that power cars will be renumbered by adding 200 to their original number.

43206 (43006)
43208 (43008)
43238 (43038)
43239 (43039)
43290 (43090)
43295 (43095)
43296 (43096)
43300 (43100)
43305 (43105)
43306 (43106)
43307 (43107)
43308 (43108)
43309 (43109)
43310 (43110)
43311 (43111)
43312 (43112)
43313 (43113)
43314 (43114)
43315 (43115)
43316 (43116)
43317 (43117)
43318 (43118)
43319 (43119)
43320 (43120)
43367 (43167)

CLASS 45　　　　　　BR/SULZER　　　　1Co-Co1

Built: 1963 by BR at Derby Locomotive Works.
Engine: Sulzer 12LDA28B of 1860 kW (2500 h.p.) at 750 r.p.m.
Main Generator: Crompton-Parkinson CG426 A1.
Traction Motors: Crompton-Parkinson C172 A1.
Maximum Tractive Effort: 245 kN (55000 lbf).
Continuous Tractive Effort: 134 kN (31600 lbf) at 22.3 m.p.h.

Power At Rail: 1490 kW (2000 h.p.).	**Train Brakes:** Air & vacuum.
Brake Force: 63 t.	**Dimensions:** 20.70 x 2.78 m.
Weight: 136 t.	**Wheel Diameter:** 914/1143 mm.
Design Speed: 90 m.p.h.	**Maximum Speed:** 90 m.p.h.
Fuel Capacity: 3591 litres.	**RA:** 6.
Train Supply: Electric, index 66.	**Multiple Working:** Not equipped.

Originally numbered D61.

45112 　**B**　FM　SDMS　　DF　　THE ROYAL ARMY ORDNANCE CORPS

CLASS 47　　　BR/BRUSH/SULZER　　　Co-Co

Built: 1963–1967 by Brush Traction, at Loughborough or by BR at Crewe Works.
Engine: Sulzer 12LDA28C of 1920 kW (2580 h.p.) at 750 r.p.m.
Main Generator: Brush TG160-60 Mk4 or TM172-50 Mk1.
Traction Motors: Brush TM64-68 Mk1 or Mk1A.
Maximum Tractive Effort: 267 kN (60000 lbf).
Continuous Tractive Effort: 133 kN (30000 lbf) at 26 m.p.h.

Power At Rail: 1550 kW (2080 h.p.).	**Train Brakes:** Air.
Brake Force: 61 t.	**Dimensions:** 19.38 x 2.79 m.
Weight: 111.5–120.6 t.	**Wheel Diameter:** 1143 mm.
Design Speed: 95 m.p.h.	**Maximum Speed:** 95 m.p.h. (* 75 m.p.h.).
Fuel Capacity: 3273 (+ 5550).	

Train Supply: Not equipped.
Multiple Working: † DRS system, m Green Circle (operational locos only).

Originally numbered in series D1100–D1111, D1500–D1999 but not in order.

Non-standard liveries/numbering:

47033 Carries no number.
47145 Dark blue with Railfreight Distribution logos.
47803 BR experimental Infrastructure livery. Yellow & white with a red stripe.
47812 Carries number D1916.
47815 Also carries number D1748.
47829 "Police" livery of white with a broad red band outlined in yellow.
47851 Also carries number D1648.
47853 "XP64 blue" with red cabside panels. Also carries number D1733.
47972 BR Central Services red & grey.

Class 47/0 (Dual-braked locos) or Class 47/2 (Air-braked locos). Standard Design. Details as above.

47033	m	**CD**	CD	CROL	GL
47053	+	**FE**	FM	SDXL	BH
47145	+m	**0**	FM	SDFL	DF	MYRDDIN EMRYS
47150	*+	**FL**	FL	DFLH	FD
47186	+	**FE**	FM	SDXL	KT
47194		**F**	WC	MBDL	CS (S)
47197	*	**FF**	P	DHLT	BA
47200	+m	**CD**	CD	CRRH	GL	The Fosse Way
47201	+	**FE**	FM	SDXL	KT
47219	+	**FE**	FM	SDXL	KT
47224	x*	**F**	P	DHLT	CP
47226	+	**F**	FM	SDXL	KT
47228	+	**FE**	FM	SDXL	KT
47229	+	**F**	FM	SDXL	BH
47236	+	**FE**	WC	MBDL	CS (S)
47237	+†	**DR**	DR	XHNC	KM
47245	+m	**WS**	WC	MBDL	CS
47270	*	**FL**	P	DHLT	BA	Cory Brothers 1842–1992
47279	*+	**FL**	P	DHLT	BA
47280	+	**F**	FM	SDXL	KT
47289	*+	**FF**	P	DHLT	BA
47292	*+	**FL**	P	DHLT	BA
47293	+	**FE**	FM	SDXL	KT
47298	+†	**DR**	DR	XHNC	KM

Class 47/3 (Dual-braked locos) or Class 47/2 (Air-braked locos).
Details as Class 47/0 except: **Weight:** 113.7 t.

47302	+	**FF**	FL	DHLT	BA
47303	*+	**FF**	P	DHLT	BA	Freightliner Cleveland
47306	+	**FE**	HN	HNRS	BZ	The Sapper
47307	+	**FE**	FM	SDXL	KT
47309	*+	**FE**	FL	DHLT	SZ	European Rail Operator of The Year
47313	+	**F**	FM	SDXL	KT
47314	+	**F**	FM	SDXL	KT
47316	+m	**CD**	CD	CRRH	OY (S) Cam Peak
47335	+	**F**	FM	SDXL	KT
47338	+	**FE**	CD	CROL	DW
47345		**FF**	WC	MBDL	LB (S)
47348	+	**FE**	FM	SDXL	MQ
47355	m	**FB**	FM	SDFL	DF	AVOCET
47358	*+	**FF**	P	DHLT	SZ	IVANHOE
47360	+	**FE**	FM	SDXL	KT
47363		**F**	FM	SDXL	CS
47368	x	**F**	FM	SDXL	CS
47370	*+	**FF**	P	DHLT	IP
47375	+	**FB**	FM	SDFL	DF (S)

Class 47/4. Electric Train Supply equipment.
Details as Class 47/0 except:

Weight: 120.4–125.1 t.   **Fuel Capacity:** 3273 (+ 5887) litres.
Train Supply: Electric. ETH 66.   **RA:** 7.

47475	x	**RX**	HN	HNRS	HM
47488	x	**GG**	FM	SDFR	BH (S)
47489	x	**RG**	FM	SDXL	CS
47492	x	**RG**	GD	MBDL	CS (S)
47501	xt	**DR**	DR	XHNC	KM
47525	x	**FE**	FM	SDXL	CS
47526	x	**BL**	FM	SDXL	CS
47528	x	**IM**	CD	CRUR	DW
47550	x	**IM**	FM	SDXL	IR
47575	x	**RG**	RV	RTLS	BQ
47635	x	**BL**	E	WNTR	OC

Class 47/7. Previously fitted with an older form of TDM.

Details as Class 47/4 except:
Weight: 118.7 t.   **Fuel Capacity:** 5887 litres.
Maximum Speed: 100 m.p.h.

47701	x	**FR**	WF	SDFR	LU (S)	Waverley
47703	x	**FR**	FM	SDFR	DF	HERMES
47707	x	**RX**	FM	SDXL	BH	
47709	x	**BP**	FM	SDFR	DF	DIONYSOS
47710	x	**FR**	FM	SDFR	DF (S)	
47712	x	**BP**	FM	SDFR	DF	ARTEMIS
47714	xm	**AR**	CD	CRRH	NC	
47715		**FR**	FM	SDXL	YK	POSEIDON
47717	x	**RG**	FM	SDXL	BH	

Class 47/7. Former Railnet dedicated locos. All have twin fuel tanks and are fitted with RCH jumper cables for operation with Propelling Control Vehicles (PCVs).

47721		**RX**	E	WNXX	TT	Saint Bede
47722		**V**	E	WNXX	TT	
47726		**RX**	E	WNXX	TT	Manchester Airport Progress
47727		**E**	E	WNTR	WN	Castell Caerffili/Caerphilly Castle
47732	x	**RX**	E	WNTR	HM	
47733		**RX**	E	WNTR	HM	
47734		**RX**	E	WNTR	HM	
47736		**RX**	E	WNXX	CD	
47737		**RX**	E	WNSS	HM	
47739		**RX**	E	WNSS	ML	
47741		**V**	E	WNXX	TT	
47742		**RX**	E	WNXX	TT	The Enterprising Scot
47744		**E**	FM	SDXL	BH	
47746		**RX**	E	WNTR	CD	
47747		**E**	E	WNTR	MH	Florence Nightingale
47749		**RX**	E	WNXX	HM	
47750		**V**	E	WNXX	HM	
47758	x	**E**	E	WNXX	TT	

47759	**RX**	E	WNXX	CD	
47760	**E**	E	WNTR	HM	
47761	**RX**	E	WNTR	MG	
47767	**E**	FM	SDXL	AS	
47769	**V**	RV	RTLO	CP	Resolve
47770	**RX**	E	WNXX	BS	Reserved
47772 x	**RX**	E	WNTR	MG	
47773	**E**	E	WNXX	HM	
47776 x	**RX**	E	WNXX	HM	
47780	**RX**	FM	SDXL	BH	
47781	**RX**	E	WNXX	TT	Isle of Iona
47782	**RX**	E	WNXX	OC	
47783	**RX**	E	WNXX	CD	
47784	**RX**	E	WNXX	CD	
47785	**E**	E	WNTR	ML	
47786	**E**	E	WNXX	HM	
47787	**E**	E	WNXX	HM	
47789	**RX**	E	WNSS	TT	
47790	**E**	E	WNTR	HM	
47791	**RX**	E	WNXX	SY	
47792	**E**	E	WNTR	HM	
47793	**E**	E	WNTR	HM	

Class 47/4 continued. RA6.

47798	**RP**	NM	MBDL	CS	Prince William
47799	**RP**	E	WNXX	FB	Prince Henry
47802 +†	**DR**	DR	XHNC	KM	
47803	**0**	X	SDXL	AS	
47805 +	**RV**	RV	XHNC	KM	TALISMAN
47810 +	**V**	CD	CRRH	NC	
47811 +	**GL**	P	DFLH	FD	
47812 +	**GG**	RV	XHNC	KM	
47813 +m	**CD**	CD	CRRH	GL	John Peel
47815 +m	**GG**	RV	RTLO	CP	GREAT WESTERN
47816 +	**GL**	P	DFLH	FD	
47818 +	**1**	CD	CRRH	GL	
47826 +	**IC**	WC	MBDL	CS	Springburn
47828 +m	**CD**	CD	CRRH	GL	Joe Strummer
47829 +	**0**	RV	RTLO	CP (S)	
47830 +	**GL**	P	DFLH	FD	
47832 +m	**FM**	FM	SDFR	DF	DRIVER TOM CLARK O.B.E.
47839 +m	**RV**	RV	XHNC	KM	PEGASUS
47840 +	**B**	P	CRRH	LB (S)	NORTH STAR
47841 +	**V**	P	DFLH	FD	
47843 +	**RV**	RV	XHNC	KM	VULCAN
47847 +m	**BL**	RV	XHNC	KM	
47848 +m	**RV**	RV	XHNC	KM	TITAN STAR
47851 +	**GG**	WC	MBDL	CS	Traction Magazine
47853 +	**0**	RV	XHNC	KM	RAIL EXPRESS
47854 +	**WS**	WC	MBDL	CS	
47972	**0**	FM	SDXL	CS	

CLASS 50   ENGLISH ELECTRIC   Co-Co

Built: 1967–1968 by English Electric at Vulcan Foundry, Newton-le-Willows.
Engine: English Electric 16CVST of 2010 kW (2700 h.p.) at 850 r.p.m.
Main Generator: English Electric 840/4B.
Traction Motors: English Electric 538/5A.
Maximum Tractive Effort: 216 kN (48500 lbf).
Continuous Tractive Effort: 147 kN (33000 lbf) at 23.5 m.p.h.

Power At Rail: 1540 kW (2070 h.p.).	**Train Brakes:** Air & vacuum.
Brake Force: 59 t.	**Dimensions:** 20.88 x 2.78 m.
Weight: 116.9 t.	**Wheel Diameter:** 1092 mm.
Design Speed: 105 m.p.h.	**Maximum Speed:** 90 m.p.h.
Fuel Capacity: 4796 litres.	**RA:** 6.
Train Supply: Electric, index 61.	**Multiple Working:** Orange Square.

Originally numbered D431 and D449.

| 50031 | **BL** | 50 | CFOL | KR | Hood |
| 50049 | **BL** | PD | CFOL | KR | Defiance |

CLASS 52   WESTERN   C-C

Built: 1961–1964 Swindon Works.
Engine: Two Maybach MD655 of 1007 kW (1350 h.p) at 1500 r.p.m.
Transmission: Hydraulic. Voith L630rV.
Maximum Tractive Effort: 297 kN (66700 lbf).
Continuous Tractive Effort: 201 kN (45200 lbf) at 14.5 m.p.h.

Power At Rail: 1490 kW (2000 h.p.).	**Train Brakes:** Air & vacuum.
Brake Force: 83 t.	**Dimensions:** 20.7 m x 2.78 m.
Weight: 110 t.	**Wheel Diameter:** 1092 mm.
Design Speed: 90 m.p.h.	**Maximum Speed:** 90 m.p.h.
Fuel Capacity: 3900 litres.	**RA:** 6.
Train Supply: Steam.	**Multiple Working:** Not equipped.

Never allocated a number in the 1972 number series.

Registered on TOPS as No. 89416.

| D1015 | **M** | DT | MBDL | OC | WESTERN CHAMPION |

CLASS 55   ENGLISH ELECTRIC   Co-Co

Built: 1961 by English Electric at Vulcan Foundry, Newton-le-Willows.
Engine: Two Napier-Deltic D18-25 of 1230 kW (1650 h.p.) each at 1500 r.p.m.
Main Generators: Two English Electric 829/1A.
Traction Motors: English Electric 538/A.
Maximum Tractive Effort: 222 kN (50000 lbf).
Continuous Tractive Effort: 136 kN (30500 lbf) at 32.5 m.p.h.

Power At Rail: 1969 kW (2640 h.p.).	**Train Brakes:** Air & vacuum.
Brake Force: 51 t.	**Dimensions:** 21.18 x 2.68 m.
Weight: 100 t.	**Wheel Diameter:** 1092 mm.
Design Speed: 105 m.p.h	**Maximum Speed:** 100 m.p.h.

Fuel Capacity: 3755 litres.
Train Supply: Electric, index 66.

RA: 5.
Multiple Working: Not equipped.

Originally numbered D9000.

Registered on TOPS as No. 89500.

55022	**B**	MW ELRD	BQ	ROYAL SCOTS GREY

CLASS 56   BRUSH/BR/PAXMAN   Co-Co

Built: 1976–1984 by Electroputere at Craiova, Romania (as sub contractors for Brush) or BREL at Doncaster or Crewe Works.
Engine: Ruston Paxman 16RK3CT of 2460 kW (3250 h.p.) at 900 r.p.m.
Main Alternator: Brush BA1101A.
Traction Motors: Brush TM73-62.
Maximum Tractive Effort: 275 kN (61800 lbf).
Continuous Tractive Effort: 240 kN (53950 lbf) at 16.8 m.p.h.
Power At Rail: 1790 kW (2400 h.p.).
Brake Force: 60 t.
Weight: 126 t.
Design Speed: 80 m.p.h.
Fuel Capacity: 5228 litres.
Train Supply: Not equipped.

Train Brakes: Air.
Dimensions: 19.36 x 2.79 m.
Wheel Diameter: 1143 mm.
Maximum Speed: 80 m.p.h.
RA: 7.
Multiple Working: Red Diamond.

Note: All equipped with Slow Speed Control.

Non-standard liveries:

56063 As **F**, but with the light grey replaced by a darker grey.
56027 and 56109 Are **LH** but with the Loadhaul branding on one side only.

56006	**B**	E	WNSS	BH
56007	**FER**	E	WZGF	FN
56011	**E**	FM	SDXL	CV
56018	**FER**	E	WZGF	FN
56021	**LH**	FM	SDXL	CV
56022	**F**	FM	SDXL	IR
56025	**F**	E	WNXX	IM
56027	**LH**	E	WNXX	IM
56029	**F**	J	RCJA	LB (S)
56031	**FER**	E	WZGF	FN
56032	**FER**	E	WZGF	FN
56033	**F**	E	WNXX	HM
56034	**LH**	J	RCJA	LB (S)
56037	**E**	E	WZTS	OC
56038	**FER**	E	WZGF	FN
56041	**E**	E	WNXX	HM
56043	**F**	E	WNXX	IM
56044	**F**	X	WNSO	LB
56046	**CE**	E	WNXX	TO
56048	**CE**	E	WZTS	HM
56049	**FER**	E	WZGF	FN
56051	**FER**	E	WZGF	DM

56052	F	E	WNXX	IM
56053	F	E	WNXX	HM
56054	F	E	WNXX	FB
56055	LH	E	WNXX	HM
56056	F	E	WNTR	HM
56058	FER	E	WZGF	FN
56059	FER	E	WZGF	FN
56060	FER	E	WZGF	FN
56061	F	FM	SDXL	BH
56062	E	E	WNSS	MG
56063	0	X	WNSO	LB
56064	F	E	WNXX	IM
56065	FER	E	WZGF	DM
56067	E	E	WNXX	FB
56068	E	E	WNXX	HM
56069	FER	E	WZGF	FN
56070	F	E	WNTR	OC
56071	FER	E	WZGF	FN
56072	F	E	WNSS	HM
56073	F	E	WNXX	TO
56074	FER	E	WZGF	FN
56076	F	E	WNXX	IM
56077	LH	E	WNXX	CD
56078	FER	E	WZGF	FN
56079	F	E	WNXX	HM
56081	FER	E	WZGF	WB
56082	F	E	WNXX	IM
56083	LH	E	WNXX	FB
56084	LH	E	WNXX	IM
56085	LH	E	WNXX	TE
56086	F	E	WNXX	IM
56087	FER	E	WZGF	FN
56088	E	E	WNSS	TE
56089	E	E	WNXX	IM
56090	FER	E	WZGF	FN
56091	FER	E	WZGF	FN
56093	F	E	WNXX	HM
56094	FER	E	WZGF	FN
56095	FER	E	WZGF	DM
56096	FER	E	WZGF	FN
56099	F	E	WNXX	HM
56100	LH	E	WNXX	MG
56101	F	E	WNXX	IM
56102	LH	E	WNXX	TE
56103	FER	E	WZGF	FN
56104	FER	E	WZGF	FN
56105	FER	E	WZGF	FN
56106	FER	E	WZGF	FN
56107	LH	E	WNTR	FB
56108	F	E	WNXX	TE
56109	LH	E	WNXX	FB

56110	**LH**	E	WNXX	HM	
56111	**LH**	E	WNXX	TE	
56112	**LH**	E	WNXX	OC	
56113	**FER**	E	WZGF	FN	
56114	**E**	E	WNTR	IM	
56115	**FER**	E	WZGF	FN	
56116	**LH**	E	WNXX	HM	
56117	**FER**	E	WZGF	DM	
56118	**FER**	E	WZGF	OC	
56119	**E**	E	WNTR	HM	
56120	**E**	E	WNXX	FB	
56127	**F**	E	WNXX	TE	
56128	**F**	HN	HNRS	LM	
56129	**F**	E	WNXX	TE	
56131	**F**	X	WNSO	LB	
56133	**F**	E	WZTS	OC	
56134	**F**	E	WZTS	HM	
56301 (56045)		**FA**	J	RCJA	RR
56302 (56124)		**FA**	J	RCJA	RR
56303 (56125)		**FA**	FM	RCJA	RR

CLASS 57   BRUSH/GM   Co-Co

Built: 1964–1965 by Brush Traction at Loughborough or BR at Crewe Works as Class 47. Rebuilt 1997–2004 by Brush Traction at Loughborough.
Engine: General Motors 12 645 E3 of 1860 kW (2500 h.p.) at 904 r.p.m.
Main Alternator: Brush BA1101D.
Traction Motors: Brush TM64-68 Mark 1 or Mark 1a.
Maximum Tractive Effort: 244.5 kN (55000 lbf).
Continuous Tractive Effort: 140 kN (31500 lbf) at ?? m.p.h.
Power at Rail: 1507 kW (2025 h.p.).   **Train Brakes:** Air.
Brake Force: 80 t.   **Dimensions:** 19.38 x 2.79 m.
Weight: 120.6 t.   **Wheel Diameter:** 1143 mm.
Design Speed: 75 m.p.h.   **Maximum Speed:** 75 m.p.h.
Fuel Capacity: 5550 litres.   **RA:** 6
Train Supply: Not equipped.   **Multiple Working:** Not equipped.

Class 57/0. No Train Supply Equipment. Rebuilt 1998–2000.

57001 (47356)	**FL**	P	DFTZ	FD	Freightliner Pioneer
57002 (47322)	**FL**	P	DFTZ	FD	Freightliner Phoenix
57003 (47317)	**FL**	P	DFTZ	FD	Freightliner Evolution
57004 (47347)	**FL**	P	DFTZ	FD	Freightliner Quality
57005 (47350)	**FL**	P	DFTZ	FD	Freightliner Excellence
57006 (47187)	**FL**	P	DFTZ	FD	Freightliner Reliance
57007 (47332)	**FL**	P	DFTZ	FD	Freightliner Bond
57008 (47060)	**FL**	P	DFTZ	FD	Freightliner Explorer
57009 (47079)	**FL**	P	DFTZ	FD	Freightliner Venturer
57010 (47231)	**FL**	P	DFTZ	FD	Freightliner Crusader
57011 (47329)	**FL**	P	DFTZ	FD	Freightliner Challenger
57012 (47204)	**FL**	P	DFTZ	FD	Freightliner Envoy

Class 57/3. Electric Train Supply Equipment. Virgin Trains locos. Rebuilt 2002–2004. Details as Class 57/0 except:

Engine: General Motors 12645F3B of 2050 kW (2750 h.p.) at 954 r.p.m.
Main Alternator: Brush BA1101F (recovered from a Class 56) or Brush BA1101G
Fuel Capacity: 5887 litres.   **Train Supply:** Electric, index 100.
Design Speed: 95 m.p.h.   **Maximum Speed:** 95 m.p.h.
Brake Force: 60 t.   **Weight:** 117 t.

57301	(47845)	d	**VT**	P	ATTB	MA	SCOTT TRACY
57302	(47827)	d	**VT**	P	ATTB	MA	VIRGIL TRACY
57303	(47705)	d	**VT**	P	ATTB	MA	ALAN TRACY
57304	(47807)	d	**VT**	P	ATTB	MA	GORDON TRACY
57305	(47822)	d	**VT**	P	ATTB	MA	JOHN TRACY
57306	(47814)	d	**VT**	P	ATTB	MA	JEFF TRACY
57307	(47225)	d	**VT**	P	ATTB	MA	LADY PENELOPE
57308	(47846)	d	**VT**	P	ATTB	MA	TIN TIN
57309	(47806)	d	**VT**	P	ATTB	MA	BRAINS
57310	(47831)	d	**VT**	P	ATTB	MA	KYRANO
57311	(47817)	d	**VT**	P	ATTB	MA	PARKER
57312	(47330)	d	**VT**	P	ATTB	MA	THE HOOD
57313	(47371)	d	**VT**	P	ATTB	MA	TRACY ISLAND
57314	(47372)	d	**VT**	P	ATTB	MA	FIREFLY
57315	(47234)	d	**VT**	P	ATTB	MA	THE MOLE
57316	(47290)	d	**VT**	P	ATTB	MA	FAB 1

Class 57/6. Electric Train Supply Equipment. Prototype ETS loco. Rebuilt 2001. Details as Class 57/0 except:

Main Alternator: Brush BA1101E.   **Fuel Capacity:** 3273 litres.
Train Supply: Electric, index 100.   **Weight:** 113 t.
Design Speed: 95 m.p.h.   **Maximum Speed:** 95 m.p.h.
Brake Force: 60 t.

57601	(47825)	**WC**	WC MBDL	CS	

Class 57/6. Electric Train Supply Equipment. First Great Western locos. Rebuilt 2004. Details as Class 57/3.

57602	(47337)	**GL**	P	IWLA	LA	Restormel Castle
57603	(47349)	**GL**	P	IWLA	LA	Tintagel Castle
57604	(47209)	**GL**	P	IWLA	LA	Pendennis Castle
57605	(47206)	**GL**	P	IWLA	LA	Totnes Castle

CLASS 58   BREL/PAXMAN   Co-Co

Built: 1983–1987 by BREL at Doncaster Works.
Engine: Ruston Paxman 12RK3ACT of 2460 kW (3300 h.p.) at 1000 r.p.m.
Main Alternator: Brush BA1101B.   **Traction Motors:** Brush TM73-62.
Maximum Tractive Effort: 275 kN (61800 lbf).
Continuous Tractive Effort: 240 kN (53950 lbf) at 17.4 m.p.h.
Power At Rail: 1780 kW (2387 h.p.).   **Train Brakes:** Air.
Brake Force: 60 t.   **Dimensions:** 19.13 x 2.72 m.
Weight: 130 t.   **Wheel Diameter:** 1120 mm.

Design Speed: 80 m.p.h.
Fuel Capacity: 4214 litres.
Train Supply: Not equipped.

Maximum Speed: 80 m.p.h.
RA: 7.
Multiple Working: Red Diamond.

Notes: All equipped with Slow Speed Control.

Locos in use in The Netherlands currently carry the following numbers: 58039; 5811, 58044; 5812 and 58038; 5814.

Non-standard liveries:

58001 As **FO** but with a red solebar stripe.
58038 Vos Logistics (black with a broad orange stripe).

58001	**O**	E	WNXX	BH	
58002	**ML**	E	WNXX	EH	
58003	**F**	E	WNXX	TO	Markham Colliery
58004	**FER**	E	WZFF	DM	
58005	**ML**	E	WZTS	TO	
58006	**F**	E	WZTS	EH	
58007	**SCO**	E	WZFF	FN	
58008	**ML**	E	WNXX	TT	
58009	**SCO**	E	WZFF	FN	
58010	**FER**	E	WZFF	FN	
58011	**FER**	E	WZFF	DM	
58012	**F**	E	WNXX	TO	
58013	**ML**	E	WZTS	EH	
58014	**ML**	E	WNXX	TT	
58015	**FER**	E	WZFF	FN	
58016	**FER**	E	WZFF	OC	
58017	**F**	E	WZTS	EH	
58018	**FER**	E	WZFF	FN	
58019	**F**	E	WNXX	TO	Shirebrook Colliery
58020	**GIF**	E	WZFS	ES	
58021	**FER**	E	WZFF	FN	
58022	**F**	E	WNXX	CD	
58023	**ML**	E	WNXX	TT	
58024	**GIF**	E	WZFS	ES	
58025	**GIF**	E	WZFS	ES	
58026	**F**	E	WZTS	EH	
58027	**SCO**	E	WZFF	FN	
58028	**F**	E	WNXX	TT	
58029	**GIF**	E	WZFS	ES	
58030	**GIF**	E	WZFS	ES	
58031	**GIF**	E	WZFS	ES	
58032	**FER**	E	WZFF	FN	
58033	**TSO**	E	WZFF	EH	
58034	**FER**	E	WZFF	FN	
58035	**FER**	E	WZFF	FN	
58036	**ML**	E	WZFH	TT	
58037	**E**	E	WNXX	EH	
58038	**O**	E	WZFH	TB	
58039	**ACT**	E	WZFH	TB	
58040	**SCO**	E	WZFF	EH	

58041	**GIF**	E	WZFS	ES
58042	**ML**	E	WNXX	EH
58043	**GIF**	E	WZFS	ES
58044	**ACT**	E	WZFH	TB
58045	**F**	E	WNXX	OC
58046	**FER**	E	WZFF	FN
58047	**TSO**	E	WZFF	EH
58048	**E**	E	WNXX	OC
58049	**TSO**	E	WZFF	FN
58050	**TSO**	E	WZFF	FN

CLASS 59   GENERAL MOTORS   Co-Co

Built: 1985 (59001/59002/59004) or 1989 (59005) by General Motors, La Grange, Illinois, USA or 1990 (59101–59104), 1994 (59201) and 1995 (59202–59206) by General Motors, London, Ontario, Canada.
Engine: General Motors 16-645E3C two stroke of 2460 kW (3300 h.p.) at 904 r.p.m.
Main Alternator: General Motors AR11 MLD-D14A.
Traction Motors: General Motors D77B.
Maximum Tractive Effort: 506 kN (113 550 lbf).
Continuous Tractive Effort: 291 kN (65 300 lbf) at 14.3 m.p.h.
Power At Rail: 1889 kW (2533 h.p.).   **Train Brakes:** Air.
Brake Force: 69 t.   **Dimensions:** 21.35 x 2.65 m.
Weight: 121 t.   **Wheel Diameter:** 1067 mm.
Design Speed: 60 (* 75) m.p.h.   **Maximum Speed:** 60 (* 75) m.p.h.
Fuel Capacity: 4546 litres.   **RA:** 7.
Train Supply: Not equipped.   **Multiple Working:** AAR System.

Class 59/0. Owned by Foster-Yeoman.

59001	**FY**	FY	XYPO	MD	YEOMAN ENDEAVOUR
59002	**FY**	FY	XYPO	MD	ALAN J DAY
59004	**FY**	FY	XYPO	MD	PAUL A HAMMOND
59005	**FY**	FY	XYPO	MD	KENNETH J PAINTER

Class 59/1. Owned by Hanson Quarry Products.

59101	**HA**	HA	XYPA	MD	Village of Whatley
59102	**HA**	HA	XYPA	MD	Village of Chantry
59103	**HA**	HA	XYPA	MD	Village of Mells
59104	**HA**	HA	XYPA	MD	Village of Great Elm

Class 59/2. Owned by EWS.

59201	*	**E**	E	WDAG	TD	Vale of York
59202	*	**E**	E	WDAG	TD	Vale of White Horse
59203	*	**E**	E	WDAG	TD	Vale of Pickering
59204	*	**E**	E	WDAG	TD	Vale of Glamorgan
59205	*b	**E**	E	WDAG	TD	L. Keith McNair
59206	*b	**E**	E	WDAG	TD	Pride of Ferrybridge

CLASS 60   BRUSH/MIRRLEES   Co-Co

Built: 1989–1993 by Brush Traction at Loughborough.
Engine: Mirrlees 8MB275T of 2310 kW (3100 h.p.) at 1000 r.p.m.
Main Alternator: Brush BA1006A.
Traction Motors: Brush TM2161A.
Maximum Tractive Effort: 500 kN (106500 lbf).
Continuous Tractive Effort: 336 kN (71570 lbf) at 17.4 m.p.h.
Power At Rail: 1800 kW (2415 h.p.).   **Train Brakes:** Air.
Brake Force: 74 (+ 62) t.   **Dimensions:** 21.34 x 2.64 m.
Weight: 129 (+ 131) t.   **Wheel Diameter:** 1118 mm.
Design Speed: 62 m.p.h.   **Maximum Speed:** 60 m.p.h.
Fuel Capacity: 4546 (+ 5225) litres.   **RA:** 7.
Train Supply: Not equipped.   **Multiple Working:** Within class.

Notes: All equipped with Slow Speed Control.

60034, 60061, 60064, 60066, 60072, 60073, 60077, 60079, 60082, 60084, 60088 and 60090 carry their names on one side only.

60500 used to carry the number 60016.

60007, 60044 and 60078 carry EWS logos on their **LH** or **ML** liveries.

60001		E	E	WNTS	TO	The Railway Observer
60002	+	E	E	WCBN	IM	High Peak
60003	+	E	E	WCBN	IM	FREIGHT TRANSPORT ASSOCIATION
60004	+	E	E	WCBN	IM	
60005	+	E	E	WNTS	TO	BP Gas Avonmouth
60006		CU	E	WNTS	TO	Scunthorpe Ironmaster
60007	+	LH	E	WCBN	IM	
60008		E	E	WCAN	IM	Sir William McAlpine
60009	+	E	E	WNTR	TO	
60010	+	E	E	WCBN	IM	
60011		ML	E	WNTS	TO	
60012	+	E	E	WNTS	TE	
60013		EG	E	WCAN	IM	Robert Boyle
60014		EG	E	WCAN	IM	Alexander Fleming
60015	+	EG	E	WCBN	IM	Bow Fell
60017	+	E	E	WCBN	IM	Shotton Works Centenary Year 1996
60018		E	E	WCAN	IM	
60019		E	E	WCAN	IM	PATHFINDER TOURS 30 YEARS OF RAILTOURING 1973–2003
60020	+	E	E	WCBN	IM	
60021	+	E	E	WCBN	IM	Star of the East
60022	+	E	E	WCBN	IM	
60023	+	E	E	WCBN	IM	
60024		E	E	WNTS	TO	
60025	+	E	E	WCBN	IM	Caledonian Paper
60026	+	E	E	WCBN	IM	
60027	+	E	E	WCBN	IM	
60028	+	EG	E	WCBN	IM	John Flamsteed
60029		E	E	WCAN	IM	Clitheroe Castle

60030	+	E	E	WCBN	IM	
60031		E	E	WCAN	IM	ABP Connect
60032		F	E	WNTR	TO	William Booth
60033	+	CU	E	WNTR	MG	Tees Steel Express
60034		EG	E	WCAN	IM	Carnedd Llewelyn
60035		E	E	WCAN	IM	
60036		E	E	WNTR	IM	GEFCO
60037	+	E	E	WNTS	MG	Aberddawan/Aberthaw
60038	+	E	E	WCBN	IM	AvestaPolarit
60039		E	E	WCAN	IM	
60040		E	E	WCAN	IM	
60041	+	E	E	WCBN	IM	
60042		E	E	WCAN	IM	The Hundred of Hoo
60043		E	E	WCAN	IM	
60044		ML	E	WCAN	IM	
60045		E	E	WCAN	IM	The Permanent Way Institution
60046	+	EG	E	WCBN	IM	William Wilberforce
60047		E	E	WCAN	IM	
60048		E	E	WCAN	IM	EASTERN
60049		E	E	WCAN	IM	
60050		E	E	WNTS	TE	
60051	+	E	E	WCBN	IM	
60052	+	E	E	WCBN	IM	Glofa Twr – The last deep mine in Wales – Tower Colliery
60053		E	E	WCAN	IM	NORDIC TERMINAL
60054	+	F	E	WCBN	IM	Charles Babbage
60055	+	EG	E	WCBN	IM	Thomas Barnardo
60056	+	EG	E	WNTS	TO	William Beveridge
60057		EG	E	WNTR	TO	Adam Smith
60058	+	E	E	WCBN	IM	
60059	+	LH	E	WCBN	IM	Swinden Dalesman
60060		EG	E	WCAN	IM	James Watt
60061		F	E	WCAN	IM	Alexander Graham Bell
60062		E	E	WCAN	IM	
60063		EG	E	WCAN	IM	James Murray
60064	+	EG	E	WNTS	IM	Back Tor
60065		E	E	WCAN	IM	Spirit of JAGUAR
60066		EG	E	WNTR	TO	John Logie Baird
60067		EG	E	WNTR	MG	James Clerk-Maxwell
60068		F	E	WNTS	TO	Charles Darwin
60069		E	E	WCAN	IM	Slioch
60070	+	F	E	WNTS	IM	John Loudon McAdam
60071	+	E	E	WCBN	IM	Ribblehead Viaduct
60072		EG	E	WCAN	IM	Cairn Toul
60073		EG	E	WCAN	IM	Cairn Gorm
60074		EG	E	WNTR	TE	
60075		E	E	WCAN	IM	
60076		EG	E	WCAN	IM	
60077	+	F	E	WNTS	IM	Canisp
60078		ML	E	WCAN	IM	
60079		EG	E	WCAN	IM	Foinaven

60080	+	E	E	WNTR	TO	
60081	+	GW	E	WNTS	TO	ISAMBARD KINGDOM BRUNEL
60082		EG	E	WCAN	IM	Mam Tor
60083		E	E	WNTR	TO	Mountsorrel
60084		F	E	WCAN	IM	Cross Fell
60085		E	E	WNTR	IM	MINI Pride of Oxford
60086		EG	E	WNTS	TO	Schiehallion
60087		E	E	WNTS	IM	Barry Needham
60088		F	E	WNTS	TO	Buachaille Etive Mor
60089	+	E	E	WNTS	IM	THE RAILWAY HORSE
60090	+	EG	E	WCBN	IM	Quinag
60091	+	EG	E	WNTR	TO	An Teallach
60092	+	EG	E	WCBN	IM	Reginald Munns
60093		E	E	WNTR	TO	
60094		E	E	WCAN	IM	Rugby Flyer
60095		EG	E	WCAN	IM	
60096	+	E	E	WCBN	IM	
60097	+	E	E	WCBN	IM	ABP Port of Grimsby & Immingham
60098	+	E	E	WNTS	IM	Charles Francis Brush
60099		EG	E	WCAN	IM	Ben More Assynt
60100		E	E	WNTR	TO	Pride of Acton
60500		E	E	WCAN	IM	RAIL Magazine

CLASS 66   GENERAL MOTORS/EMD   Co-Co

Built: 1998–2007 by General Motors/EMD, London, Ontario, Canada (Model JT42CWR (low emission locos Model JT42CWRM)).
Engine: General Motors 12N-710G3B-EC two stroke of 2385 kW (3200 h.p.) at 904 r.p.m.
Main Alternator: General Motors AR8/CA6.
Traction Motors: General Motors D43TR.
Maximum Tractive Effort: 409 kN (92000 lbf).
Continuous Tractive Effort: 260 kN (58390 lbf) at 15.9 m.p.h.
Power At Rail: 1850 kW (2480 h.p.).   **Train Brakes:** Air.
Brake Force: 68 t.   **Dimensions:** 21.35 x 2.64 m.
Weight: 126 t.   **Wheel Diameter:** 1120 mm.
Design Speed: 87.5 m.p.h.   **Maximum Speed:** 75 m.p.h.
Fuel Capacity: 6550 litres.   **RA:** 7.
Train Supply: Not equipped.   **Multiple Working:** AAR System.

Notes: All equipped with Slow Speed Control.

Class 66 delivery dates. The Class 66 design has evolved over a ten year period with over 400 of these locos now in use in the UK. For clarity the delivery dates (by year) for each batch of locos delivered to the UK is as follows:

66001–66250	EWS. 1998–2000
66401–66410	DRS. 2003
66411–66420	DRS. 2006
66501–66505	Freightliner. 1999
66506–66520	Freightliner. 2000
66521–66525	Freightliner. 2000 (66521 since scrapped).

66526–66531	Freightliner. 2001
66532–66537	Freightliner. 2001
66538–66543	Freightliner. 2001
66544–66553	Freightliner. 2001
66554	Freightliner. 2002*
66555–66566	Freightliner. 2002
66567–66574	Freightliner. 2003
66575–66577	Freightliner. 2004
66578–66581	Freightliner. 2005
66601–66606	Freightliner. 2000
66607–66612	Freightliner. 2002
66613–66618	Freightliner. 2003
66619–66622	Freightliner. 2005
66701–66707	GB Railfreight. 2001
66708–66712	GB Railfreight. 2002
66713–66717	GB Railfreight. 2003
66718–66722	GB Railfreight. 2006
66723–66727	GB Railfreight. on order
66951–66952	Freightliner. 2004

* Replacement for 66521, written off in the Great Heck accident in 2001.

Class 66/0. EWS-operated locomotives.

All fitted with Swinghead Automatic "Buckeye" Combination Couplers except 66001 and 66002.

66001	E	A	WBAN	TO	
66002	E	A	WBAN	TO	Lafarge Quorn
66003	E	A	WBAN	TO	
66004	E	A	WBAN	TO	
66005	E	A	WBAN	TO	
66006	E	A	WBAN	TO	
66007	E	A	WBAN	TO	
66008	E	A	WBAN	TO	
66009	E	A	WBAN	TO	
66010	E	A	WBEN	FN	
66011	E	A	WBAN	TO	
66012	E	A	WBAN	TO	
66013	E	A	WBAN	TO	
66014	E	A	WBAN	TO	
66015	E	A	WBAN	TO	
66016	E	A	WBAN	TO	
66017	E	A	WBAN	TO	
66018	E	A	WBAN	TO	
66019	E	A	WBAN	TO	
66020	E	A	WBAN	TO	
66021	E	A	WBAN	TO	
66022	E	A	WBEN	FN	
66023	E	A	WBAN	TO	
66024	E	A	WBAN	TO	
66025	E	A	WBAN	TO	
66026	E	A	WBAN	TO	

66027	E	A	WBAN	TO	
66028	E	A	WBAN	TO	
66029	E	A	WBEN	FN	
66030	E	A	WBAN	TO	
66031	E	A	WBAN	TO	
66032	E	A	WBEN	TO	
66033	E	A	WBAN	TO	
66034	E	A	WBAN	TO	
66035	E	A	WBAN	TO	
66036	E	A	WBEN	TO	
66037	E	A	WBAN	TO	
66038	E	A	WBEN	TO	
66039	E	A	WBAN	TO	
66040	E	A	WBAN	TO	
66041	E	A	WBAN	TO	
66042	E	A	WBAN	TO	Lafarge Buddon Wood
66043	E	A	WBAN	TO	
66044	E	A	WBAN	TO	
66045	E	A	WBAN	TO	
66046	E	A	WBAN	TO	
66047	E	A	WBAN	TO	
66048	E	A	WBAN	TO	
66049	E	A	WBEN	TO	
66050	E	A	WBAN	TO	
66051	E	A	WBAN	TO	
66052	E	A	WBEN	TO	
66053	E	A	WBAN	TO	
66054	E	A	WBAN	TO	
66055	E	A	WBLN	TO	
66056	E	A	WBLN	TO	
66057	E	A	WBLN	TO	
66058	E	A	WBLN	TO	
66059	E	A	WBLN	TO	
66060	E	A	WBAN	TO	
66061	E	A	WBAN	TO	
66062	E	A	WBAN	TO	
66063	E	A	WBAN	TO	
66064	E	A	WBAN	TO	
66065	E	A	WBAN	TO	
66066	E	A	WBAN	TO	
66067	E	A	WBAN	TO	
66068	E	A	WBAN	TO	
66069	E	A	WBAN	TO	
66070	E	A	WBAN	TO	
66071	E	A	WBAN	TO	
66072	E	A	WBAN	TO	
66073	E	A	WBAN	TO	
66074	E	A	WBAN	TO	
66075	E	A	WBAN	TO	
66076	E	A	WBAN	TO	
66077	E	A	WBAN	TO	Benjamin Gimbert G.C.

66078		E	A	WBAN	TO	James Nightall G.C.
66079		E	A	WBAN	TO	
66080		E	A	WBAN	TO	
66081		E	A	WBAN	TO	
66082		E	A	WBAN	TO	
66083		E	A	WBAN	TO	
66084		E	A	WBAN	TO	
66085		E	A	WBAN	TO	
66086		E	A	WBAN	TO	
66087		E	A	WBAN	TO	
66088		E	A	WBAN	TO	
66089		E	A	WBAN	TO	
66090		E	A	WBAN	TO	
66091		E	A	WBAN	TO	
66092		E	A	WBAN	TO	
66093		E	A	WBAN	TO	
66094		E	A	WBAN	TO	
66095		E	A	WBAN	TO	
66096		E	A	WBAN	TO	
66097		E	A	WBAN	TO	
66098		E	A	WBAN	TO	
66099	r	E	A	WBBM	TO	
66100	r	E	A	WBBM	TO	
66101	r	E	A	WBBM	TO	
66102	r	E	A	WBBM	TO	
66103	r	E	A	WBBM	TO	
66104	r	E	A	WBBM	TO	
66105	r	E	A	WBBM	TO	
66106	r	E	A	WBBM	TO	
66107	r	E	A	WBBM	TO	
66108	r	E	A	WBBM	TO	
66109		E	A	WBAN	TO	
66110	r	E	A	WBBM	TO	
66111	r	E	A	WBBM	TO	
66112	r	E	A	WBBM	TO	
66113	r	E	A	WBBM	TO	
66114	r	E	A	WBBM	TO	
66115		E	A	WBAN	TO	
66116		E	A	WBAN	TO	
66117		E	A	WBAN	TO	
66118		E	A	WBAN	TO	
66119		E	A	WBAN	TO	
66120		E	A	WBAN	TO	
66121		E	A	WBAN	TO	
66122		E	A	WBAN	TO	
66123		E	A	WBAN	TO	
66124		E	A	WBAN	TO	
66125		E	A	WBAN	TO	
66126		E	A	WBAN	TO	
66127		E	A	WBAN	TO	
66128		E	A	WBAN	TO	

66129	E	A	WBAN	TO	
66130	E	A	WBAN	TO	
66131	E	A	WBAN	TO	
66132	E	A	WBAN	TO	
66133	E	A	WBAN	TO	
66134	E	A	WBAN	TO	
66135	E	A	WBAN	TO	
66136	E	A	WBAN	TO	
66137	E	A	WBAN	TO	
66138	E	A	WBAN	TO	
66139	E	A	WBAN	TO	
66140	E	A	WBAN	TO	
66141	E	A	WBAN	TO	
66142	E	A	WBAN	TO	
66143	E	A	WBAN	TO	
66144	E	A	WBAN	TO	
66145	E	A	WBAN	TO	
66146	E	A	WBAN	TO	
66147	E	A	WBAN	TO	
66148	E	A	WBAN	TO	
66149	E	A	WBAN	TO	
66150	E	A	WBAN	TO	
66151	E	A	WBAN	TO	
66152	E	A	WBAN	TO	
66153	E	A	WBAN	TO	
66154	E	A	WBAN	TO	
66155	E	A	WBAN	TO	
66156	E	A	WBAN	TO	
66157	E	A	WBAN	TO	
66158	E	A	WBAN	TO	
66159	E	A	WBAN	TO	
66160	E	A	WBAN	TO	
66161	E	A	WBAN	TO	
66162	E	A	WBAN	TO	
66163	E	A	WBAN	TO	
66164	E	A	WBAN	TO	
66165	E	A	WBAN	TO	
66166	E	A	WBAN	TO	
66167	E	A	WBAN	TO	
66168	E	A	WBAN	TO	
66169	E	A	WBAN	TO	
66170	E	A	WBAN	TO	
66171	E	A	WBAN	TO	
66172	E	A	WBAN	TO	PAUL MELLENEY
66173	E	A	WBAN	TO	
66174	E	A	WBAN	TO	
66175	E	A	WBAN	TO	
66176	E	A	WBAN	TO	
66177	E	A	WBAN	TO	
66178	E	A	WBAN	TO	
66179	E	A	WBAN	TO	

66180	E	A	WBAN	TO	
66181	E	A	WBAN	TO	
66182	E	A	WBAN	TO	
66183	E	A	WBAN	TO	
66184	E	A	WBAN	TO	
66185	E	A	WBAN	TO	
66186	E	A	WBAN	TO	
66187	E	A	WBAN	TO	
66188	E	A	WBAN	TO	
66189	E	A	WBAN	TO	
66190	E	A	WBAN	TO	
66191	E	A	WBAN	TO	
66192	E	A	WBAN	TO	
66193	E	A	WBAN	TO	
66194	E	A	WBAN	TO	
66195	E	A	WBAN	TO	
66196	E	A	WBAN	TO	
66197	E	A	WBAN	TO	
66198	E	A	WBAN	TO	
66199	E	A	WBAN	TO	
66200	E	A	WBAN	TO	RAILWAY HERITAGE COMMITTEE
66201	E	A	WBAN	TO	
66202	E	A	WBAN	TO	
66203	E	A	WBAN	TO	
66204	E	A	WBAN	TO	
66205	E	A	WBAN	TO	
66206	E	A	WBAN	TO	
66207	E	A	WBAN	TO	
66208	E	A	WBAN	TO	
66209	E	A	WBAN	TO	
66210	E	A	WBAN	TO	
66211	E	A	WBAN	TO	
66212	E	A	WBAN	TO	
66213	E	A	WBAN	TO	
66214	E	A	WBAN	TO	
66215	E	A	WBEN	TO	
66216	E	A	WBAN	TO	
66217	E	A	WBAN	TO	
66218	E	A	WBAN	TO	
66219	E	A	WBAN	TO	
66220	E	A	WBAN	TO	
66221	E	A	WBAN	TO	
66222	E	A	WBAN	TO	
66223	E	A	WBAN	TO	
66224	E	A	WBAN	TO	
66225	E	A	WBAN	TO	
66226	E	A	WBAN	TO	
66227	E	A	WBAN	TO	
66228	E	A	WBAN	TO	
66229	E	A	WBAN	TO	
66230	E	A	WBAN	TO	

66231	E	A	WBAN	TO
66232	E	A	WBAN	TO
66233	E	A	WBAN	TO
66234	E	A	WBAN	TO
66235	E	A	WBAN	TO
66236	E	A	WBAN	TO
66237	E	A	WBAN	TO
66238	E	A	WBAN	TO
66239	E	A	WBAN	TO
66240	E	A	WBAN	TO
66241	E	A	WBAN	TO
66242	E	A	WBAN	TO
66243	E	A	WBAN	TO
66244	E	A	WBAN	TO
66245	E	A	WBAN	TO
66246	E	A	WBAN	TO
66247	E	A	WBAN	TO
66248	E	A	WBAN	TO
66249	E	A	WBAN	TO
66250	E	A	WBAN	TO

Class 66/4. Direct Rail Services-operated locomotives.
66401–66410. Porterbrook locos. Details as Class 66/0.

Advertising livery: 66405 WH Malcolm (DRS Blue with WH Malcolm logos).

66401	DS	P	XHIM	KM
66402	DS	P	XHIM	KM
66403	DS	P	XHIM	KM
66404	DS	P	XHIM	KM
66405	AL	P	XHIM	KM
66406	DS	P	XHNR	KM
66407	DS	P	XHIM	KM
66408	DS	P	XHNR	KM
66409	DS	P	XHNR	KM
66410	DS	P	XHIM	KM

66411–66420. Low emission. HBOS-owned. Details as Class 66/0 except:

Engine: EMD 12N-710G3B-U2 two stroke of 2420 kW (3245 h.p.) at 904 r.p.m.
Traction Motors: General Motors D43TRC.
Weight: 129.6 t.   **Fuel Capacity:** 6400 litres.

Advertising livery: 66411 Eddie Stobart Rail (two tone blue & white).

66411	AL	HX	XHIM	KM
66412	DS	HX	XHNR	KM
66413	DS	HX	XHNR	KM
66414	DS	HX	XHIM	KM
66415	DS	HX	XHIM	KM
66416	DS	HX	XHIM	KM
66417	DS	HX	XHIM	KM
66418	DS	HX	XHIM	KM
66419	DS	HX	XHIM	KM
66420	DS	HX	XHIM	KM

Class 66/5. Freightliner-operated locomotives. Details as Class 66/0.

Note: Freightliner have another 16 Class 66s on order (low emission locos), due for delivery in 2007, but neither the number series nor leasing company had been agreed as this book closed for press.

Advertising livery: 66522 Shanks Waste (one half of loco Freightliner green and one half Shanks' Waste light green).

66501	**FL**	P	DFGM	FD	Japan 2001
66502	**FL**	P	DFGM	FD	Basford Hall Centenary 2001
66503	**FL**	P	DFGM	FD	The RAILWAY MAGAZINE
66504	**FL**	P	DFGM	FD	
66505	**FL**	P	DFGM	FD	
66506	**FL**	H	DFHH	FD	Crewe Regeneration
66507	**FL**	H	DFRT	FD	
66508	**FL**	H	DFHH	FD	
66509	**FL**	H	DFRT	FD	
66510	**FL**	H	DFRT	FD	
66511	**FL**	H	DFRT	FD	
66512	**FL**	H	DFHH	FD	
66513	**FL**	H	DFHH	FD	
66514	**FL**	H	DFRT	FD	
66515	**FL**	H	DFRT	FD	
66516	**FL**	H	DFGM	FD	
66517	**FL**	H	DFGM	FD	
66518	**FL**	H	DFRT	FD	
66519	**FL**	H	DFHH	FD	
66520	**FL**	H	DFRT	FD	
66522	**AL**	H	DFRT	LD	
66523	**FL**	H	DFRT	FD	
66524	**FL**	H	DFHH	LD	
66525	**FL**	H	DFHH	FD	
66526	**FL**	P	DFRT	LD	Driver Steve Dunn (George)
66527	**FL**	P	DFRT	LD	Don Raider
66528	**FL**	P	DFHH	FD	
66529	**FL**	P	DFHH	FD	
66530	**FL**	P	DFHH	LD	
66531	**FL**	P	DFHH	FD	
66532	**FL**	P	DFGM	FD	P&O Nedlloyd Atlas
66533	**FL**	P	DFGM	FD	Hanjin Express/Senator Express
66534	**FL**	P	DFGM	FD	OOCL Express
66535	**FL**	P	DFGM	FD	
66536	**FL**	P	DFGM	FD	
66537	**FL**	P	DFGM	FD	
66538	**FL**	H	DFIM	FD	
66539	**FL**	H	DFIM	FD	
66540	**FL**	H	DFIM	FD	Ruby
66541	**FL**	H	DFIM	FD	
66542	**FL**	H	DFIM	FD	
66543	**FL**	H	DFIM	FD	
66544	**FL**	P	DFHG	LD	
66545	**FL**	P	DFHG	FD	

66546	**FL**	P	DFNR	FD	
66547	**FL**	P	DFNR	LD	
66548	**FL**	P	DFHG	LD	
66549	**FL**	P	DFHG	LD	
66550	**FL**	P	DFHG	LD	
66551	**FL**	P	DFHG	LD	
66552	**FL**	P	DFHG	LD	
66553	**FL**	P	DFHG	LD	Maltby Raider
66554	**FL**	H	DFHG	LD	
66555	**FL**	H	DFHG	LD	
66556	**FL**	H	DFHG	LD	
66557	**FL**	H	DFHG	FD	
66558	**FL**	H	DFHG	FD	
66559	**FL**	H	DFNR	LD	
66560	**FL**	H	DFHG	FD	
66561	**FL**	H	DFHG	FD	
66562	**FL**	H	DFHG	LD	
66563	**FL**	H	DFHG	LD	
66564	**FL**	H	DFHG	LD	
66565	**FL**	H	DFHG	LD	
66566	**FL**	H	DFHG	LD	
66567	**FL**	H	DFIM	FD	
66568	**FL**	H	DFIM	FD	
66569	**FL**	H	DFIM	FD	
66570	**FL**	H	DFIM	FD	
66571	**FL**	H	DFIM	FD	
66572	**FL**	H	DFIM	FD	
66573	**FL**	H	DFIM	FD	
66574	**FL**	H	DFIM	FD	
66575	**FL**	H	DFIM	FD	
66576	**FL**	H	DFIM	FD	Hamburg Sud Advantage
66577	**FL**	H	DFIM	FD	
66578	**FL**	H	DFIM	FD	
66579	**FL**	H	DFIM	FD	
66580	**FL**	H	DFIM	FD	
66581	**FL**	H	DFHG	FD	Sophie

66582
66583
66584
66585
66586
66587
66588
66589
66590
66591
66592
66593
66594

66595
66596
66597

Class 66/6. Freightliner-operated locomotives with modified gear ratios. Details as Class 66/0 except:

Maximum Tractive Effort: 467 kN (105080 lbf).
Continuous Tractive Effort: 296 kN (66630 lbf) at 14.0 m.p.h.
Design Speed: 65 m.p.h.   **Maximum Speed:** 65 m.p.h.

66601	FL	P	DFHH	FD	The Hope Valley
66602	FL	P	DFRT	FD	
66603	FL	P	DFRT	FD	
66604	FL	P	DFRT	FD	
66605	FL	P	DFRT	FD	
66606	FL	P	DFRT	FD	
66607	FL	P	DFHG	FD	
66608	FL	P	DFHG	FD	
66609	FL	P	DFHG	FD	
66610	FL	P	DFHG	FD	
66611	FL	P	DFHG	FD	
66612	FL	P	DFHG	FD	Forth Raider
66613	FL	H	DFHG	FD	
66614	FL	H	DFHG	FD	
66615	FL	H	DFHG	FD	
66616	FL	H	DFHG	FD	
66617	FL	H	DFHG	FD	
66618	FL	H	DFHG	FD	Railways Illustrated Annual Photographic Awards Alan Barnes
66619	FL	H	DFHG	FD	Derek W. Johnson MBE
66620	FL	H	DFHG	FD	
66621	FL	H	DFHG	FD	
66622	FL	H	DFHG	FD	

Class 66/7. GB Railfreight-operated locomotives. Details as Class 66/0.

Non-standard/Advertising liveries:

66705 **GB** livery but with the addition of "Union Jack" bodyside vinyls.
66709 Black & orange with MEDITE branding.

66701	GB	H	GBRT	WN	Whitemoor
66702	GB	H	GBRT	WN	Blue Lightning
66703	GB	H	GBRT	WN	Doncaster PSB 1981–2002
66704	GB	H	GBRT	WN	Colchester Power Signalbox
66705	GB	H	GBRT	WN	Golden Jubilee
66706	GB	H	GBRT	WN	Nene Valley
66707	GB	H	GBRT	WN	Sir Sam Fay GREAT CENTRAL RAILWAY
66708	GB	H	GBCM	WN	
66709	AL	H	GBCM	WN	Joseph Arnold Davies
66710	GB	H	GBCM	WN	
66711	GB	H	GBCM	WN	

66712	**GB**	H	GBCM	WN	Peterborough Power Signalbox
66713	**GB**	H	GBCM	WN	Forest City
66714	**GB**	H	GBCM	WN	Cromer Lifeboat
66715	**GB**	H	GBCM	WN	VALOUR – IN MEMORY OF ALL RAILWAY EMPLOYEES WHO GAVE THEIR LIVES FOR THEIR COUNTRY
66716	**GB**	H	GBCM	WN	Willesden Traincare Centre
66717	**GB**	H	GBCM	WN	Good Old Boy

66718–66727. Low emission. 66723–66727 on order. Details as Class 66/0 except:

Engine: EMD 12N-710G3B-U2 two stroke of 2420 kW (3245 h.p.) at 904 r.p.m.
Traction Motors: General Motors D43TRC.
Weight: 129.6 t.   **Fuel Capacity:** 6400 litres.

66718	**MT**	H	GBCM	WN
66719	**MT**	H	GBCM	WN
66720	**MT**	H	GBCM	WN
66721	**MT**	H	GBCM	WN
66722	**MT**	H	GBCM	WN
66723		H	
66724		H	
66725		H	
66726		H	
66727		H	

Class 66/9. Freightliner locos. Low emission "demonstrator" locos. Details as Class 66/0 except:

Engine: EMD 12N-710G3B-U2 two stroke of 2420 kW (3245 h.p.) at 904 r.p.m.
Traction Motors: General Motors D43TRC.
Weight: 129.6 t.   **Fuel Capacity:** 5150 litres.

| 66951 | **FL** | H | DFHG | FD |
| 66952 | **FL** | H | DFHG | FD |

CLASS 67 ALSTOM/GENERAL MOTORS EMD Bo-Bo

Built: 1999–2000 by Alstom at Valencia, Spain, as sub-contractors for General Motors (General Motors model JT42 HW-HS).
Engine: General Motors 12N-710G3B-EC two stroke of 2385 kW (3200 h.p.) at 904 r.p.m.
Main Alternator: General Motors AR9A/HEP7/CA6C.
Traction Motors: General Motors D43FM.
Maximum Tractive Effort: 141 kN (31770 lbf).
Continuous Tractive Effort: 90 kN (20200 lbf) at 46.5 m.p.h.
Power At Rail: 1860 kW.   **Train Brakes:** Air.
Brake Force: 78 t.   **Dimensions:** 19.74 x 2.72 m.
Weight: 90 t.   **Wheel Diameter:** 965 mm.
Design Speed: 125 m.p.h.   **Maximum Speed:** 125 m.p.h.
Fuel Capacity: 4927 litres.   **RA:** 8.
Train Supply: Electric, index 66.   **Multiple Working:** AAR System.

Note: All equipped with Slow Speed Control and Swinghead Automatic "Buckeye" Combination Couplers.

Non-standard livery: 67029 All over silver with EWS logos (EWS "Special Train").

67001	E	A	WAAK	TO	
67002	E	A	WAAK	TO	Special Delivery
67003	E	A	WAAK	TO	
67004 r	E	A	WABK	TO	Post Haste
67005	RZ	A	WAAK	TO	Queen's Messenger
67006	RZ	A	WAAK	TO	Royal Sovereign
67007 r	E	A	WABK	TO	
67008 r	E	A	WAAK	TO	
67009 r	E	A	WABK	TO	
67010	E	A	WNTS	TO	Unicorn
67011 r	E	A	WABK	TO	
67012	E	A	WAAK	TO	
67013	E	A	WAAK	TO	
67014	E	A	WAAK	TO	
67015	E	A	WAAK	TO	
67016	E	A	WAAK	TO	
67017	E	A	WAAK	TO	Arrow
67018	E	A	WAAK	TO	Rapid
67019	E	A	WAAK	TO	
67020	E	A	WAAK	TO	
67021	E	A	WAAK	TO	
67022	E	A	WAAK	TO	
67023	E	A	WAAK	TO	
67024	E	A	WNTS	TO	
67025	E	A	WAAK	TO	Western Star
67026	E	A	WAAK	TO	
67027	E	A	WAAK	TO	Rising Star
67028	E	A	WAAK	TO	
67029	0	A	WAAK	TO	
67030 r	E	A	WABK	TO	

2. ELECTRO-DIESEL & ELECTRIC LOCOMOTIVES

CLASS 73   BR/ENGLISH ELECTRIC   Bo-Bo

Electro-diesel locomotives which can operate either from a DC supply or using power from a diesel engine.

Built: 1965–1967 by English Electric Co. at Vulcan Foundry, Newton le Willows.
Engine: English Electric 4SRKT of 447 kW (600 h.p.) at 850 r.p.m.
Main Generator: English Electric 824/5D.
Electric Supply System: 750 V DC from third rail.
Traction Motors: English Electric 546/1B.
Maximum Tractive Effort (Electric): 179 kN (40000 lbf).
Maximum Tractive Effort (Diesel): 160 kN (36000 lbf).
Continuous Rating (Electric): 1060 kW (1420 h.p.) giving a tractive effort of 35 kN (7800 lbf) at 68 m.p.h.
Continuous Tractive Effort (Diesel): 60 kN (13600 lbf) at 11.5 m.p.h.
Maximum Rail Power (Electric): 2350 kW (3150 h.p.) at 42 m.p.h.
Train Brakes: Air, vacuum & electro-pneumatic († Air & electro-pneumatic).
Brake Force: 31 t.   **Dimensions:** 16.36 x 2.64 m.
Weight: 77 t.   **Wheel Diameter:** 1016 mm.
Design Speed: 90 m.p.h.   **Maximum Speed:** 90 m.p.h.
Fuel Capacity: 1409 litres.   **RA:** 6.
Train Supply: Electric, index 66 (on electric power only).
Multiple Working: SR System.

Formerly numbered E6001–E6020/E6022–E6026/E6028–E6049 (not in order).

Note: Locomotives numbered in the 732xx series are classed as 73/2 and were originally dedicated to Gatwick Express services.

Non-standard numbering: 73136 Also carries number D6043.

73103	**IM**	FM	SDXL	MQ	
73107	**FB**	FM	SDED	DF	SPITFIRE
73109	**SD**	SW	HYWD	WD	Battle of Britain 50th Anniversary
73117	**IM**	FM	SDXL	MQ	
73118 †c	**EP**	EU	GPSN	NP	
73130 †c	**EP**	EU	GPSN	NP	
73136	**B**	73	MBEL	SL	Perseverance
73141	**IM**	NR	QAED	ZR (S)	
73201 †	**SD**	SW	HYWD	WD	
73202 †	**GX**	P	IVGA	SL	Dave Berry
73203 †	**GX**	GB	GBZZ	SE	
73204 †	**GB**	GB	GBED	DF	Janice
73205 †	**GB**	GB	GBED	DF	Jeanette
73206 †	**GB**	GB	GBED	DF	Lisa
73207 †	**GX**	GB	GBZZ	TN	
73208 †	**B**	GB	GBED	DF	Kirsten

73209 †	**GB**	GB	GBED	DF	Alison
73212 †	**Y**	NR	QAED	DF	
73213 †	**Y**	NR	QAED	DF	
73235 †	**SD**	SW	HYWD	WD	

CLASS 86   BR/ENGLISH ELECTRIC   Bo-Bo

Built: 1965–1966 by English Electric Co. at Vulcan Foundry, Newton le Willows or by BR at Doncaster Works.
Electric Supply System: 25 kV AC 50 Hz overhead.
Train Brakes: Air.   **Brake Force:** 40 t.
Dimensions: 17.83 x 2.65 m.   **Weight:** 83–86.8 t.
RA: 6.   **Multiple Working:** TDM system.
Train Supply: Electric, index 66.

Formerly numbered E3101–E3200 (not in order).

Non-standard livery: 86233 BR "Electric blue" livery. Also carries number E3172.

Class 86/2. Standard design rebuilt with resilient wheels and Flexicoil suspension.

Traction Motors: AEI 282BZ axle hung.
Maximum Tractive Effort: 207 kN (46500 lbf).
Continuous Rating: 3010 kW (4040 h.p.) giving a tractive effort of 85 kN (19200 lbf) at 77.5 m.p.h.
Maximum Rail Power: 4550 kW (6100 h.p.) at 49.5 m.p.h.
Wheel Diameter: 1156 mm.   **Weight:** 85–86.2 t.
Design Speed: 125 m.p.h.   **Maximum Speed:** 100 m.p.h.

86205	**V**	H	SAXL	IR	
86212	**V**	H	SAXL	EM	
86215	**AR**	H	SAXL	SN	
86217	**AR**	H	SAXL	OY	
86218	**AR**	H	SAXL	IR	
86223	**AR**	FM	SDAC	OY (S)	Norwich Union
86226	**V**	H	SAXL	IR	
86228	**IC**	H	SAXL	CV	Vulcan Heritage
86229	**V**	H	SAXL	OY	
86230	**AR**	H	SAXL	SN	
86231	**V**	H	SAXL	OY	
86232	**AR**	H	SAXL	IR	
86233	**0**	FM	SDAC	OY	
86234	**AR**	H	SAXL	IR	
86235	**AR**	FM	SDAC	IR (S)	
86242	**AR**	H	SAXL	SN	
86245	**V**	H	SAXL	IR	
86246	**AR**	H	SAXL	IR	
86247	**V**	H	SAXL	IR	
86248	**V**	H	SAXL	ZH	Sir Clwyd/County of Clwyd
86250	**AR**	H	SAXL	OY	
86251	**V**	H	SAXL	OY	
86258	**V**	H	SAXL	LB	
86260	**AR**	H	SAXL	IR	

Class 86/4. Network Rail-owned locomotive.

Traction Motors: AEI 282AZ axle hung.
Maximum Tractive Effort: 258 kN (58000 lbf).
Continuous Rating: 2680 kW (3600 h.p.) giving a tractive effort of 89 kN (20000 lbf) at 67 m.p.h.
Maximum Rail Power: 4400 kW (5900 h.p.) at 38 m.p.h.
Wheel Diameter: 1156 mm.   **Weight:** 83–83.9 t.
Design Speed: 100 m.p.h.   **Maximum Speed:** 100 m.p.h.

86424	**RX**	NR	SDXL	AS

Class 86/5. Regeared locomotive operated by Freightliner.
Details as Class 86/4 except:
Continuous Rating: 2680 kW (3600 h.p.) giving a tractive effort of 117 kN (26300 lbf) at 67 m.p.h.
Maximum Speed: 75 m.p.h.   **Train Supply:** Electric, isolated.

86501 (86608)	**FL**	FL	DFGC	FE

Class 86/6. Freightliner-operated locomotives.
Details as Class 86/4 except:
Maximum Speed: 75 m.p.h.   **Train Supply:** Electric, isolated.

86602	**FL**	FL	DHLT	BA	
86604	**FL**	FL	DFNC	FE	
86605	**FL**	FL	DFNC	FE	
86606	**FF**	FL	DHLT	CE	
86607	**FL**	FL	DFNC	FE	
86609	**FL**	FL	DFNC	FE	
86610	**FL**	FL	DFNC	FE	
86612	**FL**	P	DFNC	FE	
86613	**FL**	P	DFNC	FE	
86614	**FF**	P	DFNC	FE	
86615	**FL**	P	DHLT	CE	Rotary International
86620	**FL**	P	DHLT	CE	Philip G Walton
86621	**FL**	P	DFNC	FE	
86622	**FF**	P	DFNC	FE	
86623	**FF**	P	DHLT	BA	
86627	**FL**	P	DFNC	FE	
86628	**FL**	P	DFNC	FE	
86632	**FL**	P	DFNC	FE	
86633	**FF**	P	DHLT	BA	
86635	**FL**	P	DHLT	BA	
86637	**FF**	P	DFNC	FE	
86638	**FL**	P	DFNC	FE	
86639	**FL**	P	DFNC	FE	

Class 86/9. Network Rail-owned locomotives. Rebuilt for use as Mobile Load Bank test locos to test Overhead Line Equipment, initially on the WCML. No. 1 end Traction Motors isolated. Can still move under own power.
Maximum Speed: 60 m.p.h.   **Train Supply:** Electric, isolated.

86901	**Y**	NR	QACL	RU	CHIEF ENGINEER
86902	**Y**	NR	QACL	RU	RAIL VEHICLE ENGINEERING

CLASS 87   BREL/GEC   Bo-Bo

Built: 1973–1975 by BREL at Crewe Works.
Electric Supply System: 25 kV AC 50 Hz overhead.
Traction Motors: GEC G412AZ frame mounted.
Maximum Tractive Effort: 258 kN (58000 lbf).
Continuous Rating: 3730 kW (5000 h.p.) giving a tractive effort of 95 kN
(21300 lbf) at 87 m.p.h.
Maximum Rail Power: 5860 kW (7860 h.p.) at 50.8 m.p.h.
Train Brakes: Air.   **Brake Force:** 40 t.
Dimensions: 17.83 x 2.65 m.   **Weight:** 83.3 t.
Wheel Diameter: 1150 mm.   **Design Speed:** 110 m.p.h.
Maximum Speed: 110 m.p.h.   **Train Supply:** Electric, index 95.
RA: 6.   **Multiple Working:** TDM system.

Non-standard livery: 87019 LNWR-style lined black.

87002	**P**	P	IWCA	WB	The AC Locomotive Group
87003	**V**	P	SBXL	LM	
87004	**V**	P	SBXL	LM	
87006	**DR**	P	IWCA	WB	
87007	**CD**	P	IWCA	WB	
87008	**CD**	P	SBXL	WB	
87009	**V**	P	SBXL	LM	
87010	**V**	P	SBXL	LM	
87011	**V**	P	SBXL	LM	
87012	**N**	X	SBXL	WB	
87013	**V**	P	SBXL	LM	
87014	**V**	P	SBXL	LM	
87017	**V**	P	SBXL	LM	
87018	**V**	P	SBXL	LM	
87019	**0**	X	SBXL	WB	
87020	**V**	P	SBXL	LM	
87021	**V**	P	SBXL	LM	
87022	**DR**	P	GBAC	WB	Cock o' the North
87023	**V**	P	SBXL	LM	
87025	**V**	P	SBXL	LM	
87026	**V**	P	SBXL	WB	
87027	**V**	P	SBXL	LM	
87028	**DR**	P	GBAC	WB	Lord President
87029	**V**	P	SBXL	LM	
87030	**V**	P	SBXL	LM	
87032	**V**	P	SBXL	LM	
87033	**V**	P	SBXL	LM	
87034	**V**	P	SBXL	LM	

CLASS 90   GEC   Bo-Bo

Built: 1987–1990 by BREL at Crewe Works (as sub contractors for GEC).
Electric Supply System: 25 kV AC 50 Hz overhead.
Traction Motors: GEC G412CY frame mounted.
Maximum Tractive Effort: 258 kN (58000 lbf).
Continuous Rating: 3730 kW (5000 h.p.) giving a tractive effort of 95 kN (21300 lbf) at 87 m.p.h.
Maximum Rail Power: 5860 kW (7860 h.p.) at 68.3 m.p.h.
Train Brakes: Air.
Brake Force: 40 t.   **Dimensions:** 18.80 x 2.74 m.
Weight: 84.5 t.   **Wheel Diameter:** 1150 mm.
Design Speed: 110 m.p.h.   **Maximum Speed:** 110 m.p.h.
Train Supply: Electric, index 95.   **RA:** 7.
Multiple Working: TDM system.

Non-standard livery: 90036 As **FE** but with a yellow roof. EWS stickers.

90001 b	**1**	P	IANA	NC	
90002 b	**1**	P	IANA	NC	
90003 b	**1**	P	IANA	NC	Raedwald of East Anglia
90004 b	**1**	P	IANA	NC	
90005 b	**1**	P	IANA	NC	Vice-Admiral Lord Nelson
90006 b	**1**	P	IANA	NC	Modern Railways Magazine/ Roger Ford
90007 b	**1**	P	IANA	NC	Sir John Betjeman
90008 b	**1**	P	IANA	NC	
90009 b	**1**	P	IANA	NC	
90010 b	**1**	P	IANA	NC	
90011 b	**1**	P	IANA	NC	Let's Go East of England
90012 b	**1**	P	IANA	NC	
90013 b	**1**	P	IANA	NC	
90014 b	**1**	P	IANA	NC	Norfolk and Norwich Festival
90015 b	**1**	P	IANA	NC	
90016	**FL**	E	DFLC	FE	
90017 b	**E**	E	WNTR	CE	
90018 b	**E**	E	WEFE	CE	
90019 b	**FS**	E	WEFE	CE	
90020 b	**E**	E	WEFE	CE	Collingwood
90021	**FE**	E	WNTS	CE	
90022	**EG**	E	WNTR	CE	Freightconnection
90023	**E**	E	WNTR	CE	
90024	**FS**	E	WEFE	CE	
90025	**F**	E	WNTR	CE	
90026	**E**	E	WEFE	CE	
90027	**F**	E	WEFE	CE	Allerton T&RS Depot
90028	**E**	E	WEFE	CE	Hertfordshire Rail Tours
90029	**E**	E	WNTR	CE	The Institution of Civil Engineers
90030	**E**	E	WNTS	CE	Crewe Locomotive Works
90031	**E**	E	WEFE	CE	The Railway Children Partnership Working For Street Children Worldwide

90032	E	E	WNTR	CE	
90033	FE	E	WNTS	CE	
90034	E	E	WEFE	CE	
90035	E	E	WEFE	CE	
90036	0	E	WEFE	CE	
90037	E	E	WNTS	CE	Spirit of Dagenham
90038	FE	E	WNTR	CE	
90039	E	E	WEFE	CE	
90040	E	E	WNTS	CE	The Railway Mission
90041	FL	P	DFLC	FE	
90042	FF	P	DFLC	FE	
90043	FF	P	DFLC	FE	Freightliner Coatbridge
90044	FF	P	DFLC	FE	
90045	FF	P	DFLC	FE	
90046	FL	P	DFLC	FE	
90047	FF	P	DFLC	FE	
90048	FF	P	DFLC	FE	
90049	FF	P	DFLC	FE	
90050	FF	P	WNTS	CE	

CLASS 91   GEC   Bo-Bo

Built: 1988–1991 by BREL at Crewe Works (as sub contractors for GEC).
Electric Supply System: 25 kV AC 50 Hz overhead.
Traction Motors: GEC G426AZ.   **Maximum Tractive Effort:**
Continuous Rating: 4540 kW (6090 h.p.) giving a tractive effort of ?? kN at ?? m.p.h.
Maximum Rail Power: 4700 kW (6300 h.p.) at ?? m.p.h.
Train Brakes: Air.
Brake Force: 45 t.   **Dimensions:** 19.41 x 2.74 m.
Weight: 84 t.   **Wheel Diameter:** 1000 mm.
Design Speed: 140 m.p.h.   **Maximum Speed:** 125 m.p.h.
Train Supply: Electric, index 95.   **RA:** 7.
Multiple Working: TDM system.

Note: Locos originally numbered in the 910xx series, but renumbered upon completion of overhauls at Bombardier, Doncaster by the addition of 100 to their original number. The exception to this rule was 91023 which was renumbered 91132.

91101	GN	H	IECA	BN	City of London
91102	GN	H	IECA	BN	Durham Cathedral
91103	GN	H	IECA	BN	County of Lincolnshire
91104	GN	H	IECA	BN	Grantham
91105	GN	H	IECA	BN	County Durham
91106	GN	H	IECA	BN	East Lothian
91107	GN	H	IECA	BN	Newark on Trent
91108	GN	H	IECA	BN	City of Leeds
91109	GN	H	IECA	BN	The Samaritans
91110	GN	H	IECA	BN	David Livingstone
91111	GN	H	IECA	BN	Terence Cuneo

91112	**GN**	H	IECA	BN	County of Cambridgeshire
91113	**GN**	H	IECA	BN	County of North Yorkshire
91114	**GN**	H	IECA	BN	St. Mungo Cathedral
91115	**GN**	H	IECA	BN	Holyrood
91116	**GN**	H	IECA	BN	Strathclyde
91117	**GN**	H	IECA	BN	Cancer Research UK
91118	**GN**	H	IECA	BN	Bradford Film Festival
91119	**GN**	H	IECA	BN	County of Tyne & Wear
91120	**GN**	H	IECA	BN	Royal Armouries
91121	**GN**	H	IECA	BN	Archbishop Thomas Cranmer
91122	**GN**	H	IECA	BN	Tam the Gun
91124	**GN**	H	IECA	BN	Reverend W Awdry
91125	**GN**	H	IECA	BN	Berwick-upon-Tweed
91126	**GN**	H	IECA	BN	York Minster
91127	**GN**	H	IECA	BN	Edinburgh Castle
91128	**GN**	H	IECA	BN	Peterborough Cathedral
91129	**GN**	H	IECA	BN	Queen Elizabeth II
91130	**GN**	H	IECA	BN	City of Newcastle
91131	**GN**	H	IECA	BN	County of Northumberland
91132	**GN**	H	IECA	BN	City of Durham

CLASS 92   BRUSH   Co-Co

Built: 1993–1996 by Brush Traction at Loughborough.
Electric Supply System: 25 kV AC 50 HZ overhead or 750 V DC third rail.
Traction Motors: Asea Brown Boveri design. Model 6FRA 7059B (Asynchronous 3-phase induction motors).
Maximum Tractive Effort: 400 kN (90 000 lbf).
Continuous Rating: 5040 kW (6760 h.p.) on AC, 4000 kW (5360 h.p.) on DC.
Maximum Rail Power: **Train Brakes:** Air.
Brake Force: 63 t.   **Dimensions:** 21.34 x 2.67 m.
Weight: 126 t.   **Wheel Diameter:** 1070 mm.
Design Speed: 140 km/h (87 m.p.h.).   **Maximum Speed:** 140 km/h (87 m.p.h.).
Train Supply: Electric, index 108 (AC), 70 (DC).
RA: 7.

92001	**E**	HX	WTAE	CE	Victor Hugo
92002	**EG**	HX	WTAE	CE	H.G. Wells
92003	**EG**	HX	WTAE	CE	Beethoven
92004	**EG**	HX	WTAE	CE	Jane Austen
92005	**EG**	HX	WTAE	CE	Mozart
92006	**EP**	SF	WNWX	CE	Louis Armand
92007	**EG**	HX	WTAE	CE	Schubert
92008	**EG**	HX	WTAE	CE	Jules Verne
92009	**EG**	HX	WTAE	CE	Elgar
92010	**EP**	SF	WNWX	CE	Molière
92011	**EG**	HX	WTAE	CE	Handel
92012	**EG**	HX	WTAE	CE	Thomas Hardy
92013	**EG**	HX	WTAE	CE	Puccini
92014	**EP**	SF	WNWX	CE	Emile Zola
92015	**EG**	HX	WTAE	CE	D.H. Lawrence

92016	**EG**	HX	WTAE	CE	Brahms
92017	**EG**	HX	WTAE	CE	Shakespeare
92018	**EP**	SF	WNWX	CE	Stendhal
92019	**EG**	HX	WTAE	CE	Wagner
92020	**EP**	EU	WNWX	CE	Milton
92021	**EP**	EU	WNWX	CE	Purcell
92022	**EP**	HX	WTAE	CE	Charles Dickens
92023	**EP**	SF	WNWX	CE	Ravel
92024	**EG**	HX	WTAE	CE	J.S. Bach
92025	**EG**	HX	WTAE	CE	Oscar Wilde
92026	**EG**	HX	WTAE	CE	Britten
92027	**EG**	HX	WTAE	CE	George Eliot
92028	**EP**	SF	WNWX	WB	Saint Saëns
92029	**EG**	HX	WNTR	CE	Dante
92030	**EG**	HX	WNTR	CE	Ashford
92031	**E**	HX	WTAE	CE	The Institute of Logistics and Transport
92032	**EP**	EU	WNWX	CE	César Franck
92033	**EP**	SF	WNWX	CE	Berlioz
92034	**EG**	HX	WTAE	CE	Kipling
92035	**EP**	HX	WNTS	CE	Mendelssohn
92036	**EG**	HX	WTAE	CE	Bertolt Brecht
92037	**EG**	HX	WTAE	CE	Sullivan
92038	**EP**	SF	WNWX	CE	Voltaire
92039	**EG**	HX	WTAE	CE	Johann Strauss
92040	**EP**	EU	WNWX	CE	Goethe
92041	**EG**	HX	WTAE	CE	Vaughan Williams
92042	**EG**	HX	WTAE	CE	Honegger
92043	**EP**	SF	WNWX	CE	Debussy
92044	**EP**	EU	WNWX	CE	Couperin
92045	**EP**	EU	WNWX	CE	Chaucer
92046	**EP**	EU	WNWX	CE	Sweelinck

▲ Fastline's three Class 56s entered service in 2006. On 12/06/06 56301 passes Slitting Mill, north of Chesterfield on the Midland "Old Road" with 4O90 11.01 Doncaster–Thamesport Intermodal, conveying just flat wagons. **Andrew Wills**

▼ Freightliner's 57004 "Freightliner Quality" heads 4O51 10.03 Cardiff Wentloog–Southampton Freightliner at Battledown, west of Basingstoke, on 01/03/06. **Brian Denton**

EWS-liveried 59205 "L. Keith McNair" passes Crofton with 7A09 06.56 Merehead–Acton loaded stone on 30/08/06.

Ron Westwater

60021 "Star of the East" is seen at Ribblehead with 6E13 12.40 Newbiggin–Knottingley empty gypsum containers on 08/09/05.

Rodney Lissenden

▲ 66240 passes Toton on 07/06/05 with an empty coal train from Ratcliffe Power Station. **Paul Shannon**

▼ GBRf Metronet-liveried 66722 is seen at Norton Hammer, just south of Sheffield, with a returning Hertfordshire Railtours charter from Deepcar to Ealing Broadway on 10/06/06. **Gavin Morrison**

▲ Special EWS Silver-liveried 67029 propells the EWS Company Train at Acton Turvill on 08/06/05. The train was running as a 12.56 Bath–Bath circular.
John Chalcraft

▼ GBRf-liveried 73209 "Alison" leads 73136 in BR Blue livery with 6G10 15.00 Purley–Eastleigh engineers' train at Worting on 19/08/06. 73204 and 73208 were on the rear.
Chris Wilson

Freightliner-liveried 86621 and 86604 cross Float Viaduct south of Carstairs with 4M74 14.10 Coatbridge–Crewe Freightliner on 03/02/06. **Ian Lothian**

▲ In unbranded DRS blue livery 87022 heads north at Hanslope Junction with 1S96 16.26 Willesden–Shieldmuir Mail (325 units) on 20/06/06. Since this photo was taken this loco has been renamed "Cock o' the North". **Dave Gommersall**

▼ Ex-works in First Group livery 90024 stands outside Toton depot on 10 August. After release from Toton the loco was used to haul First ScotRail's Caledonian Sleeper services. **Richard Tuplin**

▲ 91125 "Berwick-upon-Tweed" storms north at Eaton Lane with the 08.35 King's Cross–Leeds on 14/07/06.   **Andrew Wills**

▼ In EPS two tone grey livery with EWS vinyls 92024 "J. S. Bach" passes Longport with 4O69 14.01 Trafford Park–Dollands Moor Intermodal on 30/05/06.
Cliff Beeton

3. EUROTUNNEL LOCOMOTIVES

DIESEL LOCOMOTIVES

0001–0005   MaK   Bo-Bo

Built: 1992–1993 by MaK at Kiel, Germany (Model DE1004).
Engine: MTU 12V 396 Tc of 1180 kW (1580 h.p.) at 1800 rpm.
Main Alternator: BBC.   **Traction Motors:** BBC.
Maximum Tractive Effort: 305 kN (68600 lbf).
Continuous Tractive Effort: 140 kN (31500 lbf) at 20 mph.
Power At Rail: 750 kW (1012 h.p.).
Brake Force: 120 kN.   **Dimensions:** 16.50 x ?? x ?? m.
Weight: 84 t.   **Wheel Diameter:** 1000 mm.
Design Speed: 120 km/h.   **Maximum Speed:** 120 km/h.
Fuel Capacity: **Train Brakes:** Air.
Train Supply: Not equipped.   **Multiple Working:** Within class.

0001	**GY**	ET	EU
0002	**GY**	ET	EU
0003	**GY**	ET	EU
0004	**GY**	ET	EU
0005	**GY**	ET	EU

0031–0042   HUNSLET/SCHÖMA   0–4–0

Built: 1989–1990 by Hunslet Engine Company at Leeds as 900 mm. gauge.
Rebuilt: 1993-1994 by Schöma in Germany to 1435 mm. gauge.
Engine: Deutz of 270 kW (200 h.p.) at ???? rpm.
Transmission: Mechanical.   **Maximum Tractive Effort:**
Cont. Tractive Effort: **Power At Rail:**
Brake Force: **Dimensions:**
Weight: **Wheel Diameter:**
Design Speed: 50 km/h.   **Maximum Speed:** 50 km/h.
Fuel Capacity: **Train Brakes:** Air.
Train Supply: Not equipped.   **Multiple Working:** Not equipped.

0031	**Y**	ET	EU	FRANCES
0032	**Y**	ET	EU	ELISABETH
0033	**Y**	ET	EU	SILKE
0034	**Y**	ET	EU	AMANDA
0035	**Y**	ET	EU	MARY
0036	**Y**	ET	EU	LAWRENCE
0037	**Y**	ET	EU	LYDIE
0038	**Y**	ET	EU	JENNY
0039	**Y**	ET	EU	PACITA
0040	**Y**	ET	EU	JILL
0041	**Y**	ET	EU	KIM
0042	**Y**	ET	EU	NICOLE

ELECTRIC LOCOMOTIVES

9001–9113 BRUSH/ABB Bo-Bo-Bo

Built: 1993–2001 by Brush Traction at Loughborough.
Supply System: 25 kV AC 50 Hz overhead.
Traction Motors: Asea Brown Boveri design. Asynchronous 3-phase motors.
Model 6FHA 7059 (as built). Model 6FHA 7059C (7000 kW uprated locos).
Maximum Tractive Effort: 400kN (90 000lbf).
Continuous Rating: 5760 kW (7725 h.p.) giving a TE of 310 kN at 65 km/h.
(* Fleet being progressively upgraded to 7000 kW (9387 h.p.) and are also
being renumbered into the 98xx number series upon refurbishment).

Maximum Rail Power:	**Multiple Working:** TDM system.
Brake Force: 50 t.	**Dimensions:** 22.01 x 2.97 x 4.20 m.
Weight: 132 t.	**Wheel Diameter:** 1250 mm.
Design Speed: 175 km/h (100 m.p.h.)	**Maximum Speed:** 160 km/h (87 m.p.h.)
Train Supply: Electric.	**Train Brakes:** Air.

CLASS 9/0 and CLASS 9/8. Mixed traffic locomotives.

9001		**EB**	ET	EU	LESLEY GARRETT
9802	*	**EB**	ET	EU	STUART BURROWS
9803	*	**EB**	ET	EU	BENJAMIN LUXON
9804	*	**EB**	ET	EU	VICTORIA DE LOS ANGELES
9005		**EB**	ET	EU	JESSYE NORMAN
9006		**EB**	ET	EU	REGINE CRESPIN
9007		**EB**	ET	EU	DAME JOAN SUTHERLAND
9808	*	**EB**	ET	EU	ELISABETH SODERSTROM
9809	*	**EB**	ET	EU	FRANÇOIS POLLET
9810	*	**EB**	ET	EU	JEAN-PHILIPPE COURTIS
9011		**EB**	ET	EU	JOSÉ VAN DAM
9812	*	**EB**	ET	EU	LUCIANO PAVAROTTI
9013		**EB**	ET	EU	MARIA CALLAS
9814	*	**EB**	ET	EU	LUCIA POPP
9015		**EB**	ET	EU	LÖTSCHBERG 1913
9816	*	**EB**	ET	EU	WILLARD WHITE
9017		**EB**	ET	EU	JOSÉ CARRERAS
9018		**EB**	ET	EU	WILHELMENA FERNANDEZ
9819	*	**EB**	ET	EU	MARIA EWING
9820	*	**EB**	ET	EU	Nicolai Ghiaurov
9821	*	**EB**	ET	EU	TERESA BERGANZA
9022		**EB**	ET	EU	DAME JANET BAKER
9023		**EB**	ET	EU	DAME ELISABETH LEGGE-SCHWARZKOPF
9024		**EB**	ET	EU	GOTTHARD 1882
9825	*	**EB**	ET	EU	
9026		**EB**	ET	EU	FURKATUNNEL 1982
9027		**EB**	ET	EU	BARBARA HENDRICKS
9828	*	**EB**	ET	EU	DAME KIRI TE KANAWA
9029		**EB**	ET	EU	THOMAS ALLEN
9031		**EB**	ET	EU	

9032	**EB**	ET	EU	RENATA TEBALDI
9033	**EB**	ET	EU	MONTSERRAT CABALLE
9834 *	**EB**	ET	EU	MIRELLA FRENI
9035	**EB**	ET	EU	Nicolai Gedda
9036	**EB**	ET	EU	ALAIN FONDARY
9037	**EB**	ET	EU	GABRIEL BACQUIER
9038	**EB**	ET	EU	HILDEGARD BEHRENS
9040	**EB**	ET	EU	

CLASS 9/1. Freight Shuttle dedicated locomotives.

9101	**EB**	ET	EU
9102	**EB**	ET	EU
9103	**EB**	ET	EU
9104	**EB**	ET	EU
9105	**EB**	ET	EU
9106	**EB**	ET	EU
9107	**EB**	ET	EU
9108	**EB**	ET	EU
9109	**EB**	ET	EU
9110	**EB**	ET	EU
9111	**EB**	ET	EU
9112	**EB**	ET	EU
9113	**EB**	ET	EU

9701–9707 BRUSH/BOMBARDIER Bo-Bo-Bo

CLASS 9/7. Increased power freight shuttle dedicated locomotives.

Built: 2001–2002 by Brush Traction at Loughborough.
Supply System: 25 kV AC 50 Hz overhead.
Traction Motors: Asea Brown Boveri design. Asynchronous 3-phase motors.
Model 6FHA 7059C.
Maximum Tractive Effort: 400kN (90 000lbf).
Continuous Rating: 7000 kW (9387 h.p.).
Maximum Rail Power:
Brake Force: 50 t.
Weight: 132 t.
Design Speed: 175 km/h (100 m.p.h.)
Train Supply: Electric.

Multiple Working: TDM system.
Dimensions: 22.01 x 2.97 x 4.20 m.
Wheel Diameter: 1250 mm.
Maximum Speed: 160 km/h (87 m.p.h.)
Train Brakes: Air.

9701	**EB**	ET	EU
9702	**EB**	ET	EU
9703	**EB**	ET	EU
9704	**EB**	ET	EU
9705	**EB**	ET	EU
9706	**EB**	ET	EU
9707	**EB**	ET	EU

4. FORMER BR MAIN LINE LOCOS IN INDUSTRIAL SERVICE

Former British Rail main line locomotives considered to be in "industrial use" are now listed here. These locomotives do not currently have Network Rail engineering acceptance for operation on the National Rail network.

Number   *Other no./name*   *Location*

Class 11

12082	01553	St. Modwen Properties, Long Marston
12088		Johnson's (Chopwell), Widdrington Disposal Point, near Widdrington

Class 03

03112		Port of Boston, Boston Docks
03179	CLIVE	First Capital Connect, Hornsey, London
03196	JOYCE/GLYNIS	West Coast Railway Company, Carnforth
D2381		West Coast Railway Company, Carnforth

Class 07

07001		Creative Logistics, Salford, Manchester

Class 08

08032		Hanson Aggregates, Whatley Quarry
08054		Tarmac (Northern), Swinden Quarry, Grassington
08113	H017	RMS Locotec, Wakefield
08202		The Potter Group, Knowsley, Merseyside
08296		Hanson Aggregates, Machen Quarry, near Newport
08320	SUSAN	Imerys Clay Co., Blackpool Driers, Burngullow
08345	LOCO 3	Deanside Transit, Hillington, Glasgow
08388		Reliance Ind. Estate, Newton Heath, Manchester
08398	ANNABEL	Imerys Clay Company, Rocks Works, Bugle
08413	H040	RMS Locotec, Wakefield
08423	H011	Faber Prest Ports, Flixborough Wharf, Scunthorpe
08447		Deanside Transit, Hillington, Glasgow
08484		Felixstowe Dock & Railway Company, Felixstowe
08502	ANGIE	SembCorp Utilities Teesside, Wilton, Middlesbrough
08503		SembCorp Utilities Teesside, Wilton, Middlesbrough
08517		Wabtec Rail, Doncaster (West Yard)
08594		Wabtec Rail, Doncaster (West Yard)
08598	H016	The Potter Group, Knowsley, Merseyside
08600		A. V. Dawson, Middlesbrough
08602	004	Bombardier Transportation, Derby Works
08622	H028 7	RMS Locotec, Wakefield
08643		Foster Yeoman Quarries, Merehead Stone Terminal
08650	ISLE OF GRAIN	Foster Yeoman Quarries, Isle of Grain
08652		Hanson Aggregates, Whatley Quarry
08655		LH Group Services, Barton-under-Needwood

08668		Wabtec Rail, Doncaster
08678	ARTILA	West Coast Railway Company, Carnforth
08704		Port of Boston, Boston Docks
08728		Deanside Transit, Hillington, Glasgow
08731		Foster Yeoman Quarries, Merehead Stone Terminal
08736	LOCO 4	Deanside Transit, Hillington, Glasgow
08740		LH Group Services, Barton-under-Needwood
08743	Bryan Turner	SembCorp Utilities Teesside, Wilton, Middlesbrough
08764	003 FLORENCE	Transfesa, Tilbury Riverside Terminal, Tilbury
08774	ARTHUR VERNON DAWSON	A.V. Dawson, Middlesbrough
08780		LNWR Crewe Carriage Shed
08826		Foster Yeoman Quarries, Merehead Stone Terminal
08846	003	Bombardier Transportation, Derby Works
08870	H024	Castle Cement, Ketton, Stamford
08873		LH Group Services, Barton-under-Needwood
08903		SembCorp Utilities Teesside, Wilton, Middlesbrough
08943	PET II	Bombardier Transportation, Crewe Works

Class 20

20056	81	Corus, Appleby-Frodingham Works, Scunthorpe
20107	H010	Faber Prest Ports, Flixborough Wharf, Scunthorpe
20168	SIR GEORGE EARLE	Lafarge Blue Circle Cement, Hope

Class 56

56009		Brush Traction, Loughborough Works

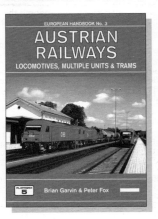

5. CODES

5.1. LIVERY CODES

Livery codes are used to denote the various liveries carried. It is impossible to list every livery variation which currently exists. In particular items ignored for this publication include:

- Minor colour variations.
- Omission of logos.
- All numbering, lettering and brandings.

Descriptions quoted are thus a general guide only. Logos as appropriate for each livery are normally deemed to be carried.

The colour of the lower half of the bodyside is stated first. Minor variations to these liveries are ignored.

Code Description

1	"One" (metallic grey with a broad black bodyside stripe. Pink, yellow, grey, pale green and light blue stripes at the unit/vehicle ends).
ACT	ACTS (Netherlands) (Deep blue with a broad yellow stripe).
AL	Advertising/promotional livery (see class heading for details).
AR	Anglia Railways (turquoise blue with a white stripe).
B	BR blue.
BL	BR Revised blue with yellow cabs, grey roof, large numbers & logo.
BP	Blue Pullman ("Nanking" blue).
BR	BR blue with a red solebar stripe.
CD	Cotswold Rail (silver with blue & red logo).
CE	BR Civil Engineers (yellow & grey with black cab doors & window surrounds).
CS	First ScotRail Caledonian Sleepers (two-tone purple with a silver stripe).
CU	Corus (silver with red logos).
DG	BR Departmental (dark grey with black cab doors & window surrounds).
DR	Direct Rail Services (dark blue with light blue or dark grey roof).
DS	Revised Direct Rail Services (dark blue, light blue & green).
E	English Welsh & Scottish Railway (maroon bodyside & roof with a broad gold bodyside band).
EB	Eurotunnel (two-tone grey with a broad blue stripe).
EG	"EWS grey". (As **F** but with large yellow & red EWS logo).
EP	European Passenger Services (two-tone grey with dark blue roof).
F	BR Trainload Freight (two-tone grey with black cab doors & window surrounds. Various logos).
FA	Fastline Freight (grey & black with white & orange stripes).
FB	Revised Fragonset {freight locos} (Black with large bodyside FRAGONSET lettering).
FD	First Group "Dynamic Lights" Inter-City (variable blue with thin multi-coloured lines on lower bodyside).
FE	Railfreight Distribution International (two tone-grey with black cab doors & dark blue roof).

FER	Fertis (light grey with a dark grey roof & solebar).
FF	Freightliner grey (two-tone grey with black cab doors & window surrounds. Freightliner logo).
FG	First Group corporate Inter-City (indigo blue with a white roof & gold, pink & white stripes).
FH	New First Great Western HST (all over indigo blue).
FL	Freightliner (dark green with yellow cabs).
FM	FM Rail (all over black with FM Rail logo).
FO	BR Railfreight (grey bodysides, yellow cabs & large BR double arrow).
FR	Fragonset Railways (black with silver roof & a red bodyside band lined out in white).
FS	First Group corporate regional/suburban (indigo blue with pink & white stripes).
FY	Foster Yeoman (blue & silver. Cast numberplates).
G	BR Green (plain green, with white stripe on main line locomotives).
GB	GB Railfreight (blue with orange cantrail & solebar stripes, orange cabs).
GG	BR green (two-tone green).
GIF	GIF (Spain) light blue with dark blue band.
GL	First Great Western locos (green with a gold stripe (no gold stripe on shunters)).
GN	Great North Eastern Railway (dark blue with a red stripe).
GS	Royal Scotsman/Great Scottish & Western Railway (maroon).
GW	Great Western Railway (green, lined out in black & orange. Cast numberplates).
GX	Gatwick Express InterCity (dark grey/white/burgundy/white).
GY	Eurotunnel (grey & yellow).
HA	Hanson Quarry Products (dark blue & silver).
HN	Harry Needle Railroad Company (orange & grey, lined out in black).
IC	BR InterCity (dark grey/white/red/white).
IM	BR InterCity Mainline (dark grey/white/red/light grey & yellow lower cabsides except shunters).
K	Black.
LH	BR Loadhaul (black with orange cabsides).
LW	LNWR black with grey & red lining.
M	BR maroon.
MA	Maintrain (blue).
ML	BR Mainline Freight (Aircraft blue with a silver stripe).
MM	Old Midland Mainline (teal green with grey lower bodyside & three tangerine stripes).
MN	New Midland Mainline (thin tangerine stripe on the lower bodyside, ocean blue, grey & white).
MT	GBRf Metronet (blue with orange cabsides).
N	BR Network South East (white & blue with red lower bodyside stripe, grey solebar & cab ends).
O	Non-standard livery (see class heading for details).
P	Porterbrook Leasing Company (purple & grey).
RG	BR Parcels (dark grey & red).
RP	Royal Train (claret, lined out in red & black).
RR	Regional Railways (dark blue/grey with light blue & white stripes, three narrow dark blue stripes at cab ends).

RT	RT Rail (black, lined out in red).
RV	Riviera Trains (Oxford blue).
RX	Rail Express Systems (dark grey & red with or without blue markings).
RZ	Royal Train revised (plain claret, no lining).
SB	Serco Railtest blue (deep blue with white Serco brandings).
SCO	Seco-Rail (orange with a broad yellow bodyside band).
SD	South West Trains outer suburban livery {Class 450 style} (deep blue, orange & red).
SL	Silverlink (indigo blue with white stripe, green lower body & yellow doors).
TSO	TSO (all over yellow with a blue solebar).
U	Plain white or grey undercoat.
V	Virgin Trains (red with black doors extending into bodysides, three white lower bodysides stripes).
VP	Virgin Trains shunters (black with a large black & white chequered flag on the bodyside).
VT	New Virgin Trains (silver with red roof. Red swept down at ends).
WA	Wabtec Rail (black).
WC	West Coast Railway Company (all over maroon with a black bodyside stripe).
WS	West Coast Railway Company {Royal Scotsman style} (all over maroon).
WX	Heart of Wessex Line promotional livery (cerise pink with various images.)
Y	Network Rail or Eurotunnel yellow.

5.2. OWNER CODES

Locomotives and rolling stock are owned by various companies and private owners and are allotted codes as follows:

Code	Owner
40	The Class 40 Preservation Society
50	The Fifty Fund
73	Class 73 Locomotive Preservation Company
A	Angel Trains
AM	Alstom
AW	Arriva Trains Wales
BT	Bombardier Transportation
CD	Cotswold Rail Engineering
CM	Cambrian Trains
DR	Direct Rail Services
DT	The Diesel Traction Group
E	English Welsh & Scottish Railway
ET	Eurotunnel
EU	Eurostar (UK)
FG	First Group
FL	Freightliner
FM	FM Rail (Fragonset Merlin Railways)
FY	Foster Yeoman

GB	GB Railfreight (owned by First Group)
GD	Garsdale Railtours
H	HSBC Rail (UK)
HA	The Hanson Group
HJ	Howard Johnston Engineering
HN	Harry Needle Railroad Company
HX	Halifax Bank of Scotland
J	Fastline (Jarvis Rail)
LW	London & North Western Railway Company
MA	Maintrain
MW	Martin Walker (Beaver Sports)
NM	National Railway Museum
NR	Network Rail
P	Porterbrook Leasing Company
PD	Project Defiance
PO	Other private owner
RT	RT Rail
RV	Riviera Trains
SF	SNCF (Société Nationale des Chemins de fer Français)
SN	Southern
SO	Serco Railtest
SW	South West Trains
TT	Type Three Traction Group
VW	Virgin West Coast
WA	Wabtec Rail
WC	West Coast Railway Company
WF	Western Falcon Rail (Alan and Tracy Lear)
X	Sold for scrap/further use and awaiting collection or owner unknown.

5.3. LOCOMOTIVE POOL CODES

Locomotives are split into operational groups ("pools") for diagramming and maintenance purposes. The official codes used to denote these pools are shown in this publication.

Code	Pool
ADFL	Advenza Freight locomotives.
ARZH	Alstom Class 08 (Glasgow Springburn).
ARZN	Alstom Class 08 (Wolverton).
ATLO	Alstom Class 08.
ATTB	Alstom Class 57.
ATXX	Alstom locos for long-term repair.
CDJD	Serco Railtest Class 08.
CFOL	Class 50 Operations Ltd.
CREL	Cotswold Rail operational locomotives – contract hire.
CROL	Cotswold Rail stored locomotives.
CRRH	Cotswold Rail operational locomotives – spot-hire contracts.
CRUR	Cotswold Rail stored locomotives – undergoing restoration.
DFGC	Freightliner Intermodal Class 86/5.
DFGM	Freightliner Intermodal Class 66.

DFHG	Freightliner Heavy Haul modified Class 66 (general).
DFHH	Freightliner Heavy Haul Class 66.
DFIM	Freightliner Intermodal modified Class 66.
DFLC	Freightliner Intermodal Class 90.
DFLH	Freightliner Heavy Haul Class 47.
DFLS	Freightliner Class 08.
DFNC	Freightliner Intermodal Class 86/6.
DFNR	Freightliner Heavy Haul modified Class 66. Infrastructure services.
DFRT	Freightliner Heavy Haul Class 66. Infrastructure services.
DFTZ	Freightliner Intermodal Class 57.
DHLT	Freightliner locomotives awaiting maintenance/repair/disposal.
ELRD	East Lancashire Railway-based main line registered locos.
GBAC	GB Railfreight Class 87.
GBCM	GB Railfreight Class 66. Railfreight contracts.
GBED	GB Railfreight Class 73.
GBRT	GB Railfreight Class 66. Network Rail contracts.
GBZZ	GB Railfreight. Stored pool.
GPSN	Eurostar (UK) Class 73.
GPSS	Eurostar (UK) Class 08.
GPSV	Eurostar (UK) Class 37.
HBSH	Wabtec hire shunting locomotives.
HGSS	Maintrain Class 08 (Tyseley/Soho)
HISE	Maintrain Class 08 (Derby).
HISL	Maintrain Class 08 (Neville Hill).
HJSE	First Great Western Class 08 (Landore).
HJSL	First Great Western Class 08 (Laira).
HJXX	First Great Western Class 08 (Old Oak HST & St. Philip's Marsh).
HNRL	Harry Needle Railroad Company hire locomotives.
HNRS	Harry Needle Railroad Company stored locomotives.
HWSU	Southern Class 09.
HYWD	South West Trains Class 73 (standby locomotives).
IANA	"One" Class 90.
IECA	Great North Eastern Railway Class 91.
IECP	Great North Eastern Railway Class 43.
IMLP	Midland Mainline Class 43.
IVGA	Gatwick Express Class 73 (standby locomotive).
IWCA	Virgin West Coast Class 87.
IWLA	First Great Western Class 57.
IWRP	First Great Western Class 43.
KCSI	Bombardier Class 08 (Ilford).
KDSD	Bombardier Class 08 (Doncaster).
MBDL	Non TOC-owned diesel locomotives.
MBEL	Non TOC-owned electric locomotives.
MOLO	RT Rail Tours locomotives.
MOLS	RT Rail Tours stored locomotives.
QACL	Network Rail Class 86.
QADD	Network Rail Class 31.
QAED	Network Rail Class 73.
QCAR	Network Rail New Measurement Train Class 43.
QETS	Network Rail stored locomotives.
RCJA	Fastline (Jarvis Rail) locomotives.

RFSH	Wabtec hire fleet.
RTLO	Riviera Trains operational fleet.
RTLS	Riviera Trains stored locomotives.
SAXL	HSBC Rail (UK) off-lease locomotives.
SBXL	Porterbrook Leasing Company off-lease locomotives.
SDAC	FM Rail Class 86.
SDED	FM Rail Class 73.
SDFL	FM Rail locomotives (freight traffic).
SDFR	FM Rail locomotives (general).
SDPP	FM Rail operational locomotives (push-pull capability).
SDMS	FM Rail museum locomotive.
SDXL	FM Rail stored locomotives.
TTTC	Type Three Traction Group Class 37.
WAAK	EWS Class 67.
WABK	EWS Class 67 RETB fitted.
WBAN	EWS Class 66 General.
WBBM	EWS Class 66 RETB fitted.
WBEN	EWS Class 66 for Euro Cargo Rail, France.
WBLN	EWS Class 66 dedicated locos for Lickey Incline banking duties. Fitted with additional lights and drawgear.
WCAN	EWS Class 60 (standard fuel tanks).
WCBN	EWS Class 60 (extended-range fuel tanks).
WDAG	EWS Class 59/2.
WEFE	EWS Class 90.
WKBM	EWS Class 37 Scotland.
WKCK	EWS Class 37 South Wales.
WNSO	EWS main line locomotives – sold awaiting collection.
WNSS	EWS main line locomotives – stored serviceable.
WNTA	EWS locomotives – stored Sandite locos.
WNTR	EWS locomotives – tactical reserve.
WNTS	EWS locomotives – tactical stored serviceable.
WNWX	EWS main line locomotives – for major repairs.
WNXX	EWS locomotives – stored unserviceable.
WNYX	EWS locomotives – authorised for component recovery.
WREM	EWS Shunting locomotives (Eastern and East Midlands – contract hire).
WRGW	EWS Shunting locomotives (Great Western and South Wales – contract hire).
WRLN	EWS shunting locomotives (North London – contract hire).
WRLS	EWS Shunting locomotives (South London – contract hire).
WRSC	EWS Shunting locomotives (Scotland and Carlisle area – contract hire).
WRWM	EWS Shunting locomotives (West Midlands and North West – contract hire).
WRWR	EWS Shunting locomotives (Western Region – contract hire).
WSAW	EWS Shunting locomotives (South Wales, on hire to Celsa).
WSEM	EWS Shunting locomotives (Eastern and East Midlands).
WSGW	EWS Shunting locomotives (Great Western and South Wales).
WSLN	EWS Shunting locomotives (North London).
WSLS	EWS Shunting locomotives (South London).
WSNE	EWS Shunting locomotives (North East).

WSSC	EWS Shunting locomotives (Scotland and Carlisle area).	
WSWM	EWS Shunting locomotives (West Midlands and North West).	
WSWR	EWS Shunting locomotives (Western Region).	
WSXX	EWS Shunting locomotives – internal/depot use.	
WTAE	EWS Class 92.	
WZFF	EWS Class 58 – hire locomotives France.	
WZFH	EWS Class 58 – hire locomotives The Netherlands.	
WZFS	EWS Class 58 – hire locomotives Spain.	
WZGF	EWS Class 56 – hire locomotives France.	
WZKF	EWS Class 37 – possible hire locomotives France.	
WZKS	EWS Class 37 – hire locomotives Spain.	
WZTS	EWS locomotives – tactical stored.	
XHIM	Direct Rail Services locomotives – Intermodal traffic.	
XHMW	Direct Rail Services locomotives undergoing long-term repairs.	
XHNC	Direct Rail Services locomotives – General.	
XHNR	Direct Rail Services locomotives – Network Rail contracts.	
XHSH	Direct Rail Services shunting locomotives.	
XHSS	Direct Rail Services stored locomotives.	
XYPA	Mendip Rail Class 59/1.	
XYPO	Mendip Rail Class 59/0.	

5.4. ALLOCATION & LOCATION CODES

Allocation codes are used in this publication to denote the normal maintenance base ("depots") of each operational locomotive. However, maintenance may be carried out at other locations and may also be carried out by mobile maintenance teams.

Location codes are used to denote common storage locations whilst the full place name is used for other locations. The designation (S) denotes stored. However, when a loco pool code denotes that a loco is stored anyway, then the (S) is not shown.

Code	Location	Depot Operator
AN	Allerton (Liverpool)	EWS
AS*	Allely's, Studley (Warwickshire)	*Storage location only*
AY	Ayr	EWS
BA	Basford Hall Yard (Crewe)	*Storage location only*
BH	Barrow Hill (Chesterfield)	Barrow Hill Engine Shed Society
BI	Brighton Lovers Walk	Southern
BK	Bristol Barton Hill	EWS
BN	Bounds Green (London)	GNER
BQ	Bury (Greater Manchester)	East Lancashire Railway
BS	Bescot (Walsall)	EWS
BY	Bletchley	Silverlink
BZ	St. Blazey (Par)	EWS
CD	Crewe Diesel (*closed*)	EWS
CE	Crewe International Electric	EWS
CF	Cardiff Canton	Arriva Trains Wales/Pullman Rail
CP	Crewe Carriage	London & North Western Railway Co.
CS	Carnforth	West Coast Railway Company

CU	Carlisle Currock	*Storage location only*
CV	Coalville Mantle Lane	FM Rail
CZ	Central Rivers (Burton)	Bombardier Transportation
DC*	Didcot Yard	EWS
DF	Derby FM Rail	FM Rail
DM*	Dollands Moor Yard	EWS
DR	Doncaster	EWS
DW*	Doncaster West Yard	*Storage location only*
DY	Derby Etches Park	Maintrain
EC	Edinburgh Craigentinny	GNER
EH	Eastleigh	EWS
EM	East Ham (London)	c2c Rail
ES*	On hire to GIF, Spain	GIF
EU*	Coquelles Eurotunnel (France)	Eurotunnel
FB	Ferrybridge (*closed*)	EWS
FD	Freightliner diesels nationwide	Freightliner
FE	Freightliner electrics nationwide	Freightliner
FN*	In use in France	Fertis/Seco-Rail/TSO or ECR
GL	Gloucester Horton Road	Cotswold Rail
HG	Hither Green (London)	EWS
HM	Healey Mills (Wakefield)	EWS
IM	Immingham	EWS
IP	Ipswich stabling point	Freightliner
IR*	Immingham Railfreight Terminal	*Storage location only*
IS	Inverness	First ScotRail
KM	Carlisle Kingmoor	Direct Rail Services
KR	Kidderminster	Severn Valley Railway
KT	MoD Kineton (Warwickshire)	Ministry of Defence
LA	Laira (Plymouth)	First Great Western
LB	Loughborough	Brush Traction
LD	Leeds Midland Road	Freightliner
LE	Landore (Swansea)	First Great Western
LL	Edge Hill (Liverpool)	West Coast Traincare
LM	Long Marston (Warwickshire)	St. Modwen Properties
LU*	MoD Ludgershall	Ministry of Defence
MA	Manchester Longsight	West Coast Traincare
MD	Merehead	Mendip Rail
MG	Margam (Port Talbot)	EWS
MH	Millerhill Yard	EWS
ML	Motherwell (Glasgow)	EWS
MO*	Mossend Yard	EWS
MQ*	Meldon Quarry (Okehampton)	*Storage location only*
MY*	Whitemoor Yard (March)	GBRf
NC	Norwich Crown Point	"One"
NL	Neville Hill (Leeds)	Maintrain/Northern
NP	North Pole International (London)	Eurostar (UK)
NW*	Brunner Mond Works, Northwich (Cheshire)	Brunner Mond
OC	Old Oak Common locomotive (London)	EWS
OO	Old Oak Common HST	First Great Western
OY	Oxley (Wolverhampton)	West Coast Traincare
PM	St. Philip's Marsh (Bristol)	First Great Western

PZ	Penzance	First Great Western
RR	Doncaster Robert's Road	Fastline
RU*	Rugby Rail Plant	Carillion Rail Plant
SB*	Sandbach Works	Albion Chemicals
SE	St. Leonards (Hastings)	St. Leonards Railway Engineering
SI	Soho (Birmingham)	Maintrain/Central Trains
SL	Stewarts Lane (London)	Gatwick Express/VSOE
SN*	MoD Shoeburyness	Ministry of Defence
SP	Springs Branch (Wigan) (*closed*)	EWS
SY	Saltley (Birmingham) (*closed*)	EWS
SZ	Southampton Maritime	Freightliner
TB*	Tilburg (Netherlands)	NedTrain
TD	Temple Mills (Stratford, London)	EWS
TE	Thornaby (Middlesbrough)	EWS
TH*	Pershore Airfield, Throckmorton, Worcs.	*Storage location only*
TM	Tyseley Locomotive Works	Birmingham Railway Museum
TN*	Tonbridge West Yard	GBRf
TO	Toton (Nottinghamshire)	EWS
TP	Trafford Park FLT	Manchester Ship Canal
TS	Tyseley (Birmingham)	Central Trains/Maintrain
TT*	Toton Training School Compound (Notts.)	*Storage location only*
TY	Tyne Yard (Newcastle)	EWS
WB	Wembley (London)	EWS
WD	Wimbledon (London)	South West Trains
WN	Willesden (London)	West Coast Traincare
WR	West Ruislip LUL	London Underground
WY	Westbury Yard	EWS
YK	National Railway Museum (York)	Science Museum
ZA	RTC Business Park (Derby)	Serco Railtest/AEA Technology
ZB	Doncaster Works	Wabtec
ZC	Crewe Works	Bombardier Transportation
ZD	Derby, Litchurch Lane Works	Bombardier Transportation
ZF	Doncaster Works	Bombardier Transportation
ZH	Springburn Works Glasgow	Alstom
ZI	Ilford Works	Bombardier Transportation
ZJ	Marcroft, Stoke	Turners
ZK	Kilmarnock Works	Hunslet Barclay
ZN	Wolverton Works	Alstom
ZR	York (former Thrall Works)	Network Rail

*= unofficial code.